The IPO Roadmap (From Private Company to Public Listing)

Step-by-Step Process of Taking a Company Public Through Traditional IPOs

By Joe Correa

Published by Live Stronger Faster

This book is for educational and informational purposes only. The author and publisher are not engaged in rendering legal, financial, or other professional advice. Readers should consult a qualified professional before making any financial decisions.

First Edition

Table of Contents

Table of Contents

Introduction

The journey from private company to publicly traded corporation is one of the most transformative events in modern business. It represents far more than simply listing shares on a stock exchange. Going public changes the structure of a company, expands access to capital, creates liquidity opportunities, attracts institutional investors, and positions a business for long-term global expansion. For many entrepreneurs, founders, executives, and investors, an Initial Public Offering (IPO) is viewed as the ultimate milestone in business growth because it turns years of effort, risk, innovation, and persistence into measurable enterprise value that can create lasting wealth for generations.

Yet despite the fascination surrounding IPOs, many business owners do not fully understand the actual process involved in taking a company public. The media often highlights billion-dollar valuations, ringing the opening bell on the stock exchange, and sudden founder wealth creation, but the reality behind a successful IPO is far more strategic, technical, and disciplined. Companies do not simply decide to go public overnight. In most cases, years of planning, financial preparation, operational scaling, legal structuring, governance improvements, investor positioning, and market timing are required before a company is ready to enter public markets successfully.

This book was created to provide a practical, realistic, and step-by-step roadmap for understanding how companies move from being privately held businesses to publicly traded corporations. Whether you are an entrepreneur building a startup, a small business owner scaling operations, an investor trying to understand capital markets, or a professional seeking insight into IPO strategy, this book is designed to simplify the process and provide clarity around one of the most important financial transitions a company can make.

Many founders mistakenly believe that IPOs are only for massive technology companies or billion-dollar corporations. While some of the most famous IPOs involve global brands, the reality is that businesses across multiple industries pursue public listings. Healthcare companies, manufacturing firms, software companies, financial institutions, consumer brands, biotechnology startups, artificial intelligence companies, logistics firms, energy businesses, and many other sectors have all successfully entered public markets. The path may vary depending on company size, market conditions, and business structure, but the core principles of becoming a publicly traded company remain surprisingly consistent. One of the most important realities to understand is that an IPO is not simply a fundraising event. It is a transition into a completely different level of business operation. Public companies face increased reporting requirements, regulatory oversight, shareholder expectations, analyst scrutiny, and quarterly performance pressure. The standards required to operate successfully as a public company are significantly higher than those required for most private businesses. This is why preparation matters so much. A poorly prepared IPO can damage a company's reputation, reduce valuation, weaken investor confidence, and create long-term operational problems. On the other hand, a well-executed IPO can create extraordinary momentum, unlock growth capital, strengthen brand credibility, and provide founders with long-term wealth-building opportunities that would otherwise be impossible.

The traditional IPO process itself involves many moving parts. Investment banks, attorneys, auditors, institutional investors, regulators, stock exchanges, analysts, and executive leadership teams all play critical roles during the process. A company preparing for an IPO must create audited financial statements, prepare registration documents, improve corporate governance, establish investor relations strategies, determine valuation targets, conduct roadshows, negotiate underwriting agreements, and satisfy regulatory requirements before shares are offered to the public. Each stage introduces risks, opportunities, costs, and strategic decisions that can dramatically influence the outcome of the offering.

This book aims to break down each of these stages into understandable concepts and actionable insights. Instead of overwhelming readers with technical jargon or legal complexity, the goal is to provide a structured roadmap that explains how the IPO process works from beginning to end. You will learn how companies determine whether they are ready to go public, how underwriters evaluate businesses, how valuation is established, how investor demand influences pricing, and how leadership teams navigate the intense preparation required before listing shares on a public exchange.

An important concept that will appear throughout this book is the relationship between growth and credibility. Public investors are not simply buying shares in a company's current performance. They are buying into a company's future potential. Investors want to see evidence of sustainable growth, scalable systems, strong leadership, competitive advantages, financial transparency, and long-term market opportunity. Companies that succeed in public markets are often those that can clearly communicate a compelling vision while simultaneously demonstrating disciplined execution and operational maturity. This is particularly important because IPOs are heavily influenced by perception and confidence.

Public markets react not only to financial performance but also to leadership quality, market timing, macroeconomic conditions, industry trends, competitive positioning, and investor sentiment. A company may have strong products and revenue growth, but if investors lack confidence in management or market sustainability, valuation can suffer significantly. Conversely, companies with strong strategic narratives and scalable business models may attract significant investor enthusiasm even before profitability reaches mature levels.

Throughout history, IPOs have played a major role in wealth creation. Many of the world's wealthiest entrepreneurs built fortunes through equity ownership in publicly traded companies. Public offerings have created liquidity for founders, employees, early investors, venture capital firms, and institutional stakeholders. Beyond personal wealth creation, IPOs also contribute to economic expansion by providing companies with access to large pools of capital that can be used for innovation, hiring, acquisitions, infrastructure development, and international growth.

For entrepreneurs, understanding the IPO process can fundamentally change the way they build businesses. A founder who understands how public investors evaluate companies will often structure operations differently from the beginning. They may prioritize scalable systems, recurring revenue models, financial reporting discipline, intellectual property protection, operational transparency, and strategic market positioning earlier in the company lifecycle. In many ways, preparing for a future IPO can improve the overall quality and value of a business long before it actually enters public markets.

At the same time, not every company should pursue an IPO. Going public introduces costs, responsibilities, and pressures that may not align with every founder's goals or business model. Some companies thrive as privately held businesses with long-term ownership stability and operational flexibility. Others benefit from private equity funding, strategic acquisitions, or alternative liquidity paths. Part of understanding the IPO roadmap involves understanding whether becoming a public company is truly the best strategic move for a particular business.

Another critical theme explored in this book is timing. Market conditions can dramatically influence IPO outcomes. During periods of strong investor confidence and economic expansion, IPO markets tend to become highly active, with elevated valuations and strong demand for growth companies. During economic downturns or periods of uncertainty, IPO activity often slows significantly as investors become more cautious.

Understanding market cycles, investor psychology, and economic conditions is essential for maximizing the probability of a successful public offering. Technology has also transformed public markets in recent decades. The rise of artificial intelligence, cloud computing, software-as-a-service models, fintech, biotechnology, digital platforms, and global internet connectivity has created entirely new categories of IPO candidates. Today, startups can scale faster than ever before, access global audiences rapidly, and achieve valuations that would have been unimaginable in previous generations. However, faster growth also creates higher expectations, stronger competition, and increased pressure to demonstrate sustainable long-term profitability.

In many ways, the IPO process forces a company to mature rapidly. Financial systems must become more sophisticated. Leadership teams must strengthen communication skills. Internal controls must improve. Compliance standards must increase. Strategic planning must become more disciplined. Public companies are expected to operate with transparency and accountability because they are managing investor capital and public trust. The companies that embrace these requirements often emerge stronger, more scalable, and more resilient than they were before going public.

This book will guide you through the core stages of the IPO journey, including preparation, valuation, underwriting, regulatory filings, investor presentations, pricing, listing execution, and post-IPO realities. You will learn how traditional IPOs differ from alternative public listing methods, how founders manage equity ownership and dilution, how public markets influence business strategy, and how long-term wealth is created through capital markets participation.

You will also gain insight into the mindset required to navigate this process successfully. Taking a company public is rarely a smooth or simple experience. It requires patience, adaptability, strategic thinking, resilience, and the ability to make difficult decisions under pressure. Many companies encounter delays, valuation changes, regulatory obstacles, or shifting market conditions during the IPO process. Success often depends not only on financial performance but also on leadership discipline and long-term vision.

The road to becoming a public company is demanding, but for the right businesses, it can unlock extraordinary opportunities. Access to institutional capital, enhanced market credibility, global brand visibility, acquisition currency, and shareholder liquidity can dramatically accelerate long-term business growth. Founders who understand how to navigate this process strategically may position themselves not only for financial success but also for lasting influence within their industries.

As you move through this book, remember that the IPO itself is not the final destination. It is a transition point. The true challenge begins after the company becomes public. Sustaining growth, managing investor expectations, maintaining operational discipline, and continuing to innovate are what ultimately determine whether a public company succeeds over the long term. The IPO opens the door, but long-term execution determines the outcome.

The purpose of this book is not merely to explain technical procedures. It is to help you understand the broader strategic, financial, and psychological dynamics that shape public market success. Whether your goal is to build a future public company, invest more intelligently, advise businesses, or simply understand how wealth is created through capital markets, the lessons within this roadmap can provide valuable insight into one of the most powerful financial systems in the modern economy.

The public markets have created some of the greatest business success stories in history. They have transformed startups into global giants, turned founders into billionaires, funded innovation across industries, and reshaped the global economy. Understanding how this process works is no longer reserved only for investment bankers or Wall Street professionals. In today's world, entrepreneurs, investors, and ambitious business owners all benefit from understanding how capital markets operate and how companies strategically position themselves for long-term growth and wealth creation.

This book is your roadmap into that world.

Chapter 1

Understanding the IPO Journey from Private Company to Public Corporation

The decision to take a company public is one of the most important strategic moves a business can make. It represents a transition from private ownership into the world of public markets, institutional investors, regulatory oversight, and large-scale capital access. While many entrepreneurs dream about launching a successful Initial Public Offering, very few fully understand the complexity, preparation, discipline, and long-term vision required to complete the process successfully. The IPO journey is not simply a financial event. It is a transformation of the company itself. The business evolves from a privately controlled operation into a publicly accountable corporation with shareholders, reporting obligations, governance structures, and market expectations that influence nearly every aspect of the organization.

Most companies begin as small private businesses with limited resources and a simple mission. A founder identifies a problem in the market, develops a solution, builds a product or service, and attempts to generate revenue. During the early stages, the company is usually funded through personal savings, friends and family contributions, small business loans, angel investors, or early-stage venture capital. At this point, the company's primary goal is survival. Founders focus heavily on product development, customer acquisition, operations, and cash flow management because the business is still proving that its model can succeed in the marketplace.

As the business begins to grow, leadership priorities gradually shift. The company may expand into new markets, hire additional employees, build management teams, improve technology infrastructure, and pursue larger funding rounds to accelerate growth. During this stage, investors begin evaluating the company not only based on current revenue but also on scalability, market opportunity, competitive advantage, recurring income potential, and future profitability. Companies that demonstrate strong growth potential often attract venture capital firms, private equity groups, or strategic institutional investors who believe the business may eventually become a public company.

The transition from private company to IPO candidate typically happens when leadership believes the business has reached a level of maturity capable of supporting public market expectations. Public investors generally expect companies to demonstrate strong revenue growth, operational stability, transparent financial reporting, scalable systems, and experienced management teams. The company must also prove that there is sufficient investor demand for its shares and that public market financing will support future growth objectives more effectively than private funding alternatives.

One of the most misunderstood aspects of an IPO is the role of capital. Many founders assume the primary purpose of going public is simply to raise money. While capital raising is certainly important, the benefits of an IPO extend far beyond financing. Public companies gain access to liquidity, improved brand visibility, acquisition opportunities through stock issuance, institutional investor participation, analyst coverage, and increased credibility within their industries. Public status can also improve recruiting efforts because employees may receive stock options or equity incentives tied directly to company performance.

However, these advantages come with significant responsibilities. Once a company becomes public, it enters a highly regulated environment that requires extensive transparency and accountability. Public companies must file quarterly and annual financial reports, disclose material events, maintain internal controls, comply with securities laws, and answer to shareholders who closely monitor company performance. Leadership teams often face intense pressure to meet quarterly expectations, maintain growth momentum, and satisfy institutional investors who may hold significant ownership stakes in the company.

For this reason, preparation is one of the most critical elements of the IPO journey. Companies that attempt to go public too early often struggle after listing because their systems, leadership structures, or financial controls are not fully developed. Successful IPO candidates usually spend years strengthening operations before filing for a public offering. They improve accounting systems, establish corporate governance structures, hire experienced executives, prepare audited financial statements, and create long-term strategic plans designed to support sustainable public market growth.

The IPO process itself usually begins with internal evaluation. Leadership teams, board members, and advisors analyze whether the company is truly ready for public markets. This evaluation includes financial performance reviews, market opportunity analysis, operational readiness assessments, competitive positioning studies, and regulatory compliance preparation. Investment banks are often brought into discussions early because they help determine whether investor demand is likely to support a successful public offering.

Investment banks play a central role in traditional IPOs. These institutions act as underwriters, helping companies structure offerings, determine valuation ranges, market shares to institutional investors, and facilitate the transition into public markets. Underwriters conduct extensive due diligence because they assume responsibility for helping distribute company shares to investors. They evaluate financial performance, growth trends, leadership quality, legal risks, market conditions, and overall business sustainability before agreeing to support an offering.

One of the most important concepts during the IPO journey is valuation. A company's valuation determines how much investors are willing to pay for ownership shares. Valuation is influenced by many factors, including revenue growth, profitability, industry trends, intellectual property, customer acquisition metrics, recurring revenue stability, market expansion opportunities, and investor sentiment. High-growth companies often receive premium valuations because investors anticipate future earnings expansion. However, inflated valuations can also create problems if future growth fails to meet expectations.

The IPO timeline can vary significantly depending on company complexity, industry regulations, market conditions, and organizational readiness. Some companies spend several years preparing for public markets, while others accelerate the process more rapidly. During preparation, financial audits become extremely important because public investors require confidence in the accuracy and transparency of financial statements. Independent auditors examine company records to ensure compliance with accounting standards and identify potential risks or inconsistencies.

Corporate governance also becomes a major priority during the IPO process. Public companies are expected to maintain independent boards of directors, ethical compliance systems, risk management procedures, and clear executive accountability structures. Governance frameworks help protect shareholders and improve investor confidence because they reduce the likelihood of financial misconduct or operational instability.

Another major component of the IPO journey involves regulatory filings. In the United States, companies seeking public listings typically file registration documents with the Securities and Exchange Commission (SEC). These filings contain detailed information about the company's financial condition, risks, operations, leadership, market strategy, and offering structure. Investors use these documents to evaluate whether the company represents an attractive investment opportunity.

The registration process can be highly demanding because regulators carefully review disclosures to ensure investors receive accurate information. Companies must disclose potential risks, legal issues, financial uncertainties, competitive threats, and operational challenges that could influence future performance. Transparency is critical because public investors rely on this information when making investment decisions.

Once regulatory filings are underway, companies begin preparing for investor presentations commonly known as roadshows. During roadshows, executives meet with institutional investors to explain the company's vision, growth strategy, financial performance, and long-term opportunities. Investor confidence plays a major role in IPO success because demand ultimately influences pricing and market performance after listing.

The psychology of public markets is another important aspect of the IPO journey. Investors are not simply evaluating financial statements. They are evaluating leadership credibility, future market potential, competitive positioning, and the company's ability to execute long-term growth plans. Strong storytelling combined with measurable operational performance often helps companies attract institutional investor support.

Timing also matters significantly. Companies frequently monitor market conditions carefully before launching IPOs. During strong economic environments with high investor optimism, public offerings may achieve higher valuations and stronger trading activity. During periods of uncertainty, inflation concerns, geopolitical instability, or recession fears, IPO markets may weaken substantially. Even strong companies sometimes delay public offerings until market conditions improve.

One reason IPOs attract so much attention is because they create opportunities for wealth creation through equity ownership. Founders, employees, early investors, and venture capital firms may all benefit financially when a company successfully enters public markets. Equity that was previously illiquid becomes tradeable on stock exchanges, allowing stakeholders to monetize portions of their ownership positions over time.

However, the transition into public markets also changes company culture. Private companies often operate with greater flexibility, secrecy, and entrepreneurial speed. Public companies face increased scrutiny from analysts, shareholders, regulators, media organizations, and competitors. Leadership teams must balance long-term innovation with short-term market expectations, which can create tension between growth strategy and quarterly performance pressure. For founders, going public can be emotionally challenging as well. Many entrepreneurs spend years building companies with full operational control, only to discover that public ownership introduces new levels of accountability and reduced decision-making independence. Shareholders expect transparency, profitability, growth discipline, and governance standards that may differ significantly from startup culture.

Despite these challenges, successful IPOs can create transformational opportunities for businesses. Public capital allows companies to expand internationally, acquire competitors, invest heavily in research and development, improve infrastructure, strengthen branding, and scale operations at levels often impossible through private financing alone. Public companies may also gain advantages in recruiting because stock-based compensation can attract highly skilled employees motivated by equity appreciation potential.

Technology and globalization have also reshaped the IPO landscape in recent decades. Today, companies can scale rapidly through digital platforms, cloud computing, artificial intelligence, and global internet connectivity. Businesses may achieve billion-dollar valuations far earlier than companies in previous generations because modern technology allows faster market penetration and operational scaling.

At the same time, competition has intensified. Public investors now analyze companies using sophisticated metrics related to recurring revenue, customer retention, user engagement, software margins, scalability efficiency, and market dominance potential. Companies seeking IPO success must often demonstrate both strong financial growth and strategic market positioning capable of sustaining future expansion.

Understanding the IPO journey requires recognizing that going public is not a single event but rather a long-term strategic evolution. Companies that succeed in public markets usually develop strong operational foundations long before filing for an IPO. They prioritize leadership quality, financial transparency, scalable systems, governance discipline, and investor communication throughout the growth process.

The companies that ultimately thrive after public listing are often those that view the IPO not as an ending, but as the beginning of a new stage of business development. Public markets provide access to capital and visibility, but long-term success still depends on execution, innovation, adaptability, and leadership discipline. A successful IPO may create opportunity, but sustainable growth determines whether a company becomes a lasting public market success story.

As this book continues, you will learn about each stage of the IPO roadmap in greater detail, including preparation strategies, valuation techniques, underwriting structures, regulatory filings, investor relations, pricing mechanisms, and post-IPO wealth management concepts. Understanding these components will provide a clearer picture of how companies strategically move from private ownership into the world of public capital markets.

The IPO journey is ultimately about transformation. It is the process through which businesses evolve from entrepreneurial ventures into institutional organizations capable of competing on a global financial stage. For founders willing to prepare carefully, scale intelligently, and lead strategically, the transition into public markets can become one of the most powerful wealth-building and business expansion opportunities available in modern finance.

From Garage Startup to Wall Street: The Rise of Apex Dynamics

When Daniel Reyes started Apex Dynamics from the small garage behind his rented home, he had no idea that one day he would stand in New York City preparing to ring the opening bell at the stock exchange. At the time, his world was far smaller. He had an old folding table, two outdated laptops, a whiteboard covered with handwritten ideas, and less than six thousand dollars remaining in his savings account. The company itself was nothing more than a software concept designed to help small logistics companies optimize delivery routes using artificial intelligence. Daniel believed the technology could save businesses time, fuel costs, and operational waste, but belief alone did not guarantee success.

The first year was brutal. Daniel worked nearly eighteen hours a day while trying to keep the company alive. During the mornings, he cold-called transportation companies attempting to secure small pilot contracts. During afternoons, he wrote software code himself because he could not afford developers. At night, he studied competitors, researched artificial intelligence models, and attempted to improve the platform's performance. Some days he questioned whether the business would survive another month.

Investors were not interested initially. Most venture capital firms ignored him completely. Some rejected him within minutes of hearing his pitch. Others believed the logistics industry was too competitive and dominated by larger corporations with far greater resources. Daniel heard the same phrases repeatedly. "Too early." "Not scalable." "Insufficient traction." "No proven market demand."

Still, Daniel refused to quit. He believed the future of transportation and logistics would depend heavily on artificial intelligence, automation, and predictive optimization systems. He understood that while large corporations already had advanced systems, small and mid-sized transportation businesses remained underserved. These companies desperately needed affordable technology solutions capable of improving efficiency without requiring massive infrastructure investments.

The breakthrough finally came during the company's second year. A regional trucking company agreed to test Apex Dynamics' software on a small fleet of delivery vehicles. Within ninety days, fuel costs declined by nearly twelve percent, delivery efficiency improved significantly, and overtime expenses fell sharply. The results immediately attracted attention from other transportation operators in the region.

Word spread faster than Daniel expected. Soon, Apex Dynamics began signing contracts with multiple logistics firms across several states. Revenue started growing rapidly. Daniel hired his first employees, rented a small office space, and expanded product development. The company still faced constant financial pressure, but for the first time, Daniel felt momentum beginning to build.

As the business grew, new challenges emerged. Managing employees proved far more difficult than building software. Customer support demands increased daily. Infrastructure costs expanded rapidly as more companies joined the platform. Investors who once ignored Apex Dynamics suddenly began requesting meetings.

Daniel eventually secured venture capital funding from a mid-sized investment firm specializing in transportation technology. The funding allowed Apex Dynamics to hire engineers, improve cybersecurity systems, expand sales operations, and accelerate product development. More importantly, it provided credibility. Once institutional investors became involved, larger clients began taking the company more seriously.

Over the next several years, Apex Dynamics expanded aggressively. The software platform evolved beyond route optimization into predictive logistics analytics, warehouse efficiency systems, and fleet management automation. Revenue climbed dramatically each year. The company expanded internationally and established partnerships with major shipping firms. Financial media outlets began referring to Apex Dynamics as one of the fastest-growing logistics technology companies in North America.

Despite the success, Daniel remained cautious. He understood that rapid growth alone did not guarantee long-term survival. Competitors were emerging quickly, and public market investors expected consistent execution. The company needed stronger financial controls, experienced leadership, governance systems, and scalable operational discipline if it hoped to become a lasting industry leader.

One afternoon, during a board meeting with investors and advisors, the conversation shifted toward the possibility of an Initial Public Offering. Daniel sat quietly while investment bankers explained the opportunity. Public markets could provide hundreds of millions of dollars in growth capital. The company could expand globally, pursue acquisitions, strengthen technology infrastructure, and increase market visibility dramatically.

But the bankers also warned about the pressure. Public companies faced constant scrutiny. Quarterly earnings expectations could influence stock performance heavily. Regulatory filings would expose detailed company information. Analysts, investors, and financial media would monitor every operational decision.

Daniel spent months debating the decision internally. Going public had once seemed like an impossible dream. Now it represented a real possibility. After extensive discussions with advisors, investors, attorneys, and executives, the board approved the decision to begin IPO preparation.

The process consumed nearly every aspect of the company. Auditors reviewed years of financial records. Attorneys prepared registration filings. Governance committees were established. Independent board members joined the organization. Investor relations teams were hired. Financial projections underwent intense analysis. Investment banks worked closely with executives to determine valuation targets and offering structures.

For Daniel, the roadshow became one of the most intense experiences of his life. He traveled constantly between cities meeting institutional investors, pension funds, hedge funds, and asset managers. Every presentation required precision. Investors challenged growth assumptions, questioned profitability timelines, analyzed competition, and evaluated leadership credibility.

Some meetings went exceptionally well. Others felt hostile and skeptical. Daniel quickly learned that public market investors viewed companies differently from venture capital firms. They cared deeply about scalability, operational discipline, margins, risk management, and long-term profitability potential.

As investor demand increased, confidence around the IPO strengthened. The underwriters eventually recommended a higher pricing range due to strong institutional interest. Financial media outlets began covering the offering heavily, describing Apex Dynamics as one of the most anticipated technology IPOs of the year.

The night before the public listing, Daniel barely slept. He sat alone in his hotel room overlooking the city skyline thinking about the journey that brought him there. He remembered the garage office, the rejection emails, the unpaid bills, the uncertainty, and the exhaustion. He remembered moments when failure seemed almost certain.

The next morning, executives, employees, investors, and advisors gathered at the stock exchange. Television cameras surrounded the trading floor while reporters discussed the offering live across financial networks. Daniel stood beside his leadership team staring at the massive electronic display showing Apex Dynamics' ticker symbol for the first time.

When the opening bell rang, applause erupted throughout the room.

Within hours, the stock price surged significantly above the IPO offering price as institutional demand exceeded expectations. The company's valuation climbed into the billions. Early investors celebrated massive returns. Employees holding stock options realized life-changing financial gains. Daniel himself officially became one of the wealthiest entrepreneurs in the transportation technology industry. Yet amid the excitement, Daniel understood something many people overlooked. The IPO was not the finish line. It was the beginning of an entirely new challenge.

In the weeks following the listing, pressure intensified immediately. Analysts issued performance expectations. Shareholders demanded continued growth. Competitors responded aggressively. Media scrutiny increased daily. Every earnings report, acquisition decision, and leadership move influenced public perception and stock performance.

Daniel eventually realized that the true test of leadership was not building a startup into an IPO candidate. The true challenge was sustaining growth, protecting shareholder trust, and continuing to innovate after entering public markets.

Years later, Daniel often spoke to entrepreneurs about the IPO journey. Many expected him to focus on wealth creation or stock market success, but his advice remained surprisingly simple.

"Going public magnifies who you already are," he would say. "If your systems are weak, public markets expose them. If your leadership lacks discipline, investors notice immediately. But if you build a real company with strong foundations, transparency, vision, and execution, public markets can accelerate your impact beyond anything you imagined." For Daniel, the IPO was never truly about money. It was about transformation. It was proof that a small idea built with persistence, discipline, and long-term vision could evolve into something capable of competing on the world stage.

Chapter 2

Evaluating Whether Your Company Is Ready for an IPO

One of the most important questions a founder or executive team can ask is whether their company is truly ready to become publicly traded. Many businesses are attracted to the idea of an Initial Public Offering because of the visibility, capital access, prestige, and wealth creation opportunities associated with public markets. However, going public before a company is operationally, financially, and strategically prepared can create serious long-term problems. Public markets reward disciplined businesses that demonstrate scalability, transparency, leadership maturity, and sustainable growth. Companies that rush into the IPO process without proper preparation often face valuation declines, shareholder dissatisfaction, operational instability, and public scrutiny that can damage the business permanently.

Readiness for an IPO is not determined by one single factor. Revenue alone does not make a company ready. A large customer base alone is not enough. Even rapid growth may not guarantee successful public market performance. IPO readiness is the result of multiple systems, financial structures, leadership qualities, governance standards, operational controls, and strategic positioning working together cohesively. The companies that perform best after going public are usually the ones that spent years preparing before they ever filed registration documents with regulators.

The first major factor in IPO readiness is financial performance. Public investors expect companies to demonstrate measurable business traction and a credible path toward long-term sustainability. While some growth companies may still operate at temporary losses, investors still want evidence that the business model itself is scalable and capable of eventually generating consistent profitability. Strong revenue growth, improving margins, predictable recurring income, and healthy unit economics all contribute to investor confidence.

Financial transparency is equally important. Private companies often operate with flexible accounting systems and limited reporting requirements. Public companies cannot function this way. Investors, regulators, analysts, and institutional shareholders require accurate, audited, and transparent financial statements. This means a company preparing for an IPO must implement strong accounting systems capable of producing reliable financial data consistently. Independent audits become essential because investors must trust the accuracy of reported numbers before committing capital. Another critical readiness factor is revenue consistency. Investors generally prefer companies with stable and predictable growth patterns rather than businesses heavily dependent on unpredictable sales cycles or one-time transactions. Recurring revenue models, subscription services, long-term contracts, and diversified customer bases often attract stronger investor interest because they create more financial stability and visibility into future performance.

Scalability also plays a major role in IPO readiness. Investors are not simply evaluating what a company has achieved already. They are evaluating what the company could become over the next five to ten years. Businesses capable of expanding rapidly without proportionally increasing expenses tend to receive higher valuations because scalability creates the potential for stronger future profitability. Technology companies, software platforms, digital marketplaces, and subscription-based models often attract premium valuations because they can scale globally while maintaining relatively efficient cost structures.

Leadership quality is another major factor investors examine carefully. Public companies require experienced executives capable of operating within highly competitive and regulated environments. Investors evaluate whether leadership teams possess strategic vision, operational discipline, communication skills, financial understanding, and the ability to manage large organizations effectively. Founders who successfully lead startups during early growth stages may still need additional executive support before entering public markets.

This is one reason many IPO-bound companies hire experienced executives prior to going public. Chief Financial Officers with public company experience become particularly valuable because they understand regulatory compliance, investor relations, reporting requirements, and capital markets strategy. Public companies also benefit from leadership teams capable of communicating effectively with institutional investors, analysts, media organizations, and shareholders.

Corporate governance is another area that significantly influences IPO readiness. Public companies are expected to operate with accountability, transparency, and oversight structures designed to protect shareholders. This includes forming boards of directors, establishing independent board committees, implementing compliance systems, and creating clear reporting structures. Governance weaknesses can severely damage investor confidence because they increase the perceived risk of operational failures or financial misconduct.

Operational infrastructure is equally important. Companies preparing for IPOs must evaluate whether their systems can support large-scale growth and public market expectations. This includes technology systems, cybersecurity protections, supply chain management, customer support operations, legal compliance procedures, human resources infrastructure, and risk management frameworks. Weak operational systems often become major liabilities once a company faces public scrutiny.

Market positioning also influences IPO readiness significantly. Investors want to understand whether the company has a defendable competitive advantage. Businesses operating in crowded markets without differentiation may struggle to attract strong investor interest. Companies with unique technology, intellectual property, strong branding, network effects, industry leadership, or proprietary systems often perform better because they possess clearer long-term growth potential.

Timing matters as well. A company may be fundamentally strong but still delay an IPO because of unfavorable market conditions. Economic uncertainty, rising interest rates, geopolitical instability, declining investor sentiment, or weak sector performance can reduce public market demand for new offerings. Smart leadership teams monitor market cycles carefully and often adjust IPO timing strategically to maximize valuation and investor participation.

An often-overlooked factor in IPO readiness is company culture. Public companies operate differently from startups. Employees must adapt to increased accountability, regulatory oversight, and performance expectations. Internal communication structures become more formalized. Decision-making processes may slow due to compliance requirements. Leadership teams must determine whether the company culture can evolve successfully without losing innovation and operational efficiency.

Another important consideration is legal readiness. Public companies face significantly higher legal exposure than private businesses. Regulatory filings, investor disclosures, securities laws, intellectual property protection, employment compliance, and contractual obligations all become increasingly important. Companies preparing for IPOs usually work extensively with securities attorneys to reduce legal risks before entering public markets.

Risk management becomes another critical area of focus during IPO preparation. Investors expect companies to identify and manage operational, financial, cybersecurity, regulatory, and market-related risks effectively. Weak risk management systems can create major concerns during investor due diligence because public shareholders want confidence that leadership can navigate future challenges successfully.

One of the most difficult aspects of evaluating IPO readiness involves understanding investor perception. Internal leadership teams may feel emotionally attached to the company and view the business optimistically, but institutional investors evaluate companies objectively based on growth potential, financial performance, industry trends, and competitive positioning. Investment banks often help companies assess how public investors are likely to view the business.

This process usually includes valuation modeling, investor sentiment analysis, industry comparisons, and market positioning studies. Companies are often compared against publicly traded competitors to determine whether investors are likely to support the proposed offering valuation. Understanding these comparisons can help leadership teams identify weaknesses that need improvement before entering public markets.

Cash flow management is another major component of IPO readiness. Even high-growth companies can fail if they manage cash inefficiently. Investors evaluate whether the company can fund operations sustainably while continuing to invest in expansion. Excessive debt, poor expense controls, or weak capital allocation strategies can reduce investor confidence significantly.

Another area companies must evaluate carefully is shareholder structure. Overly complicated ownership structures, unresolved equity disputes, excessive dilution, or unclear voting rights can create problems during IPO preparation. Public investors generally prefer clean ownership structures with transparent governance and clearly defined shareholder rights.

Brand reputation also matters more than many founders realize. Public companies operate under constant media attention and public scrutiny. Negative publicity, unresolved lawsuits, ethical controversies, cybersecurity breaches, or customer dissatisfaction can damage investor confidence rapidly. Companies preparing for IPOs often invest heavily in public relations, brand management, and reputation strengthening before entering public markets.

Employee readiness is equally important. IPOs create major organizational transitions that affect compensation structures, stock options, reporting requirements, and company culture.

Employees must understand how public markets operate and how their responsibilities may evolve after listing. Internal alignment becomes critical because operational disruptions during IPO transitions can harm company performance.

One of the most valuable exercises during IPO preparation is conducting internal stress testing. Leadership teams analyze how the business would perform under various market conditions, growth slowdowns, economic recessions, operational disruptions, or investor pressure scenarios. Public markets can become volatile quickly, and companies must demonstrate resilience under pressure.

Companies also need to evaluate whether they truly need public capital. Some businesses achieve strong growth through private equity funding, venture capital, strategic partnerships, or internal cash flow generation. Going public introduces significant costs and responsibilities, so leadership teams must determine whether public markets align with long-term strategic goals.

An IPO should never be pursued solely for prestige or media attention. Companies that succeed in public markets usually pursue IPOs because public capital supports expansion strategies, acquisitions, research and development, infrastructure growth, or long-term market leadership objectives. Strategic alignment matters significantly because public shareholders expect disciplined capital allocation after listing.

Readiness also requires emotional discipline from leadership. Public markets create constant pressure. Stock prices fluctuate daily. Analysts issue performance opinions regularly. Investors question decisions aggressively during earnings calls. Leadership teams must remain focused on long-term execution despite short-term market volatility and public criticism.

Many successful public companies spent years preparing quietly before launching IPOs. They improved governance systems, strengthened balance sheets, diversified revenue streams, upgraded operational infrastructure, hired experienced executives, and refined strategic positioning long before announcing plans to go public. These companies understood that preparation creates stability, and stability creates investor confidence.

The IPO readiness process ultimately forces companies to examine themselves honestly. Weaknesses that may be manageable in private environments become magnified in public markets. Operational inefficiencies, leadership gaps, financial inconsistencies, governance weaknesses, and strategic uncertainty can quickly undermine public investor trust.

At the same time, preparing for an IPO can strengthen a company significantly even if it never ultimately goes public. The discipline required for IPO readiness often improves operational efficiency, financial transparency, leadership structure, strategic planning, and organizational accountability. Many companies become stronger businesses simply by preparing for public market standards. Evaluating IPO readiness is therefore not just about determining whether a company can go public. It is about determining whether the organization is capable of sustaining long-term success within the demanding environment of public capital markets. Companies that approach this process strategically and honestly position themselves for stronger valuations, smoother transitions, and more sustainable growth after listing.

The road to becoming a public company begins long before registration filings or investor roadshows. It begins with preparation, discipline, operational maturity, and the willingness to build a business capable of thriving under the intense expectations of public markets.

The Decision That Changed TitanGrid Technologies Forever

Sophia Martinez stared silently through the glass conference room overlooking downtown Austin as the leadership team debated the future of TitanGrid Technologies. Five years earlier, the company had operated from a cramped warehouse office with fewer than ten employees. Now, TitanGrid had grown into one of the fastest-rising energy software firms in the country, helping utility companies manage electrical grid efficiency through predictive artificial intelligence systems.

Revenue had exploded over the past three years. Major utility providers signed multi-million-dollar contracts with the company. Venture capital firms aggressively competed for ownership stakes. Financial media outlets began describing TitanGrid as a future IPO candidate. Employees whispered constantly about stock options and future wealth. Yet despite the excitement surrounding the company, Sophia felt deeply uncertain.

The board wanted to begin preparing for an Initial Public Offering.

“Market conditions are favorable,” one investment advisor explained confidently. “Institutional investors are actively looking for AI infrastructure companies. If we move now, valuation demand could be enormous.”

Several executives nodded enthusiastically.

"Our growth numbers are strong," the Chief Revenue Officer added. "If we delay too long, competitors could catch up."

Sophia remained quiet.

She understood the opportunity. Public markets could provide hundreds of millions of dollars in expansion capital. TitanGrid could acquire smaller competitors, expand internationally, build larger data centers, and accelerate product development dramatically. But she also understood something many people in the room underestimated. TitanGrid was growing fast, but parts of the company still felt fragile beneath the surface.

Customer support systems were overloaded. Internal accounting processes remained inconsistent. Cybersecurity protections needed improvement. Employee turnover had increased as the company scaled rapidly. Several large contracts depended heavily on a small number of enterprise clients. Public markets would expose every weakness instantly.

That evening, Sophia sat alone in her office reviewing operational reports long after everyone else left. She remembered the early days of the company vividly. She had founded TitanGrid after witnessing repeated energy inefficiencies while working for a regional utility provider. Her vision was simple: use artificial intelligence to modernize electrical grid management and reduce energy waste across the country.

The first years were incredibly difficult. Investors initially dismissed the idea because utility companies were known for slow technology adoption. Sophia exhausted nearly all her personal savings trying to keep the company alive. She worked weekends consulting for other businesses just to fund payroll during difficult months.

Everything changed after TitanGrid successfully reduced outage prediction failures for a mid-sized energy provider in Texas. The software identified infrastructure weaknesses before breakdowns occurred, saving the client millions of dollars in emergency repair costs. The success attracted attention quickly.

Soon, utility companies across multiple states began adopting TitanGrid's systems. Revenue climbed rapidly. Venture capital funding followed. The company expanded from twelve employees to nearly four hundred within four years.

Now Wall Street was calling.

The next morning, Sophia scheduled private meetings with department heads throughout the company. Instead of discussing valuation or investor demand, she asked deeper questions.

"Are our systems truly ready for public scrutiny?"

The responses worried her.

The cybersecurity director admitted that infrastructure improvements were still underway. The accounting department revealed that quarterly reporting systems remained partially manual. Human resources struggled to manage rapid hiring demands. Customer service managers warned about operational strain as enterprise contracts expanded. Sophia realized the company had focused heavily on growth while postponing structural improvements necessary for long-term stability.

Several weeks later, the board reconvened with investment bankers present. Financial projections suggested the IPO could value TitanGrid at nearly six billion dollars.

"This market window may not stay open forever," one banker warned. "Investors are enthusiastic right now."

Sophia leaned forward calmly.

"If we go public today," she said, "our valuation might be high initially. But if our infrastructure breaks under pressure six months later, public markets will punish us far more aggressively than private investors ever could."

The room became silent.

Some board members looked frustrated. Others listened carefully.

Sophia continued.

"We are building a long-term company, not chasing a temporary stock market event. I would rather delay the IPO and become truly ready than rush into public markets unprepared."

The decision shocked many investors.

Instead of launching the IPO immediately, Sophia spent the next two years strengthening TitanGrid internally. The company upgraded cybersecurity systems, automated financial reporting, diversified enterprise contracts, expanded governance structures, improved operational controls, and recruited experienced executives with public company backgrounds.

The process was expensive and exhausting. Some investors became impatient. Competitors attempted to capitalize on the delay. Financial media occasionally questioned whether TitanGrid had missed its opportunity.

But internally, the company became far stronger.

Employees gained clearer organizational structures. Customer retention improved dramatically. Financial systems became highly transparent. Operational efficiency increased significantly. Leadership teams developed more discipline around forecasting, compliance, and scalability.

By the time TitanGrid officially filed for its IPO, the company looked completely different than it had two years earlier.

Institutional investors noticed immediately.

During roadshow presentations, analysts praised the company's operational maturity, governance discipline, financial transparency, and long-term scalability. Investor demand exceeded expectations rapidly. The offering became oversubscribed within days.

When TitanGrid finally entered public markets, the company launched successfully with strong institutional backing and long-term investor confidence. More importantly, the business continued performing well after listing because the underlying systems were prepared for public market pressure.

Months later, a financial journalist asked Sophia during an interview why she delayed the IPO despite favorable market conditions years earlier.

Her answer became widely quoted across business media.

"Public markets don't just reward growth," she said. "They reward companies that can survive growth."

Years later, TitanGrid became one of the most respected energy infrastructure technology firms in the world. The company expanded internationally, acquired competitors, and continued innovating within renewable energy systems and AI infrastructure management.

Sophia often reflected on the decision that changed everything.

The IPO itself created wealth, visibility, and opportunity. But the real success came from understanding that readiness mattered more than timing alone. By strengthening the company before entering public markets, TitanGrid gained something far more valuable than a temporary valuation spike.

It gained durability.

And in the world of public companies, durability often determines which businesses survive long enough to become legendary.

Months later, a financial journalist asked Sophia during an interview why she delayed the IPO despite favourable market conditions years earlier.

Her answer became widely quoted across business media.

"Public markets don't just reward growth," she said. "They reward companies that can survive growth."

Years later, TitanGrid became one of the most respected energy infrastructure technology firms in the world. The company expanded internationally, acquired competitors, and continued innovating within renewable energy systems and AI infrastructure management.

Sophia often reflected on the decision that changed everything.

The IPO itself created wealth, visibility, and opportunity. But the real success came from understanding that readiness mattered more than timing alone. By strengthening the company before entering public markets, TitanGrid gained something far more valuable than temporary valuation spikes.

It gained durability.

And in the world of public companies, durability often determines which businesses survive long enough to become legendary.

Chapter 3

Building the Financial Foundation Required for a Successful IPO

One of the most critical elements of a successful Initial Public Offering is the financial foundation supporting the company. Public investors may be inspired by innovation, growth potential, branding, or market disruption, but ultimately, public markets rely heavily on financial confidence. Investors want proof that a company understands its numbers, controls its operations, manages risk effectively, and possesses the financial discipline necessary to operate as a public corporation. Without a strong financial foundation, even the most exciting business ideas can struggle to gain investor trust.

Many private companies focus heavily on growth during their early stages. Startups often prioritize customer acquisition, product development, marketing expansion, and rapid scaling. While aggressive growth can attract attention, public investors eventually begin asking deeper questions. Is the revenue sustainable? Are margins improving? Is customer acquisition efficient? Can the company eventually produce strong profits? Are financial reports accurate and transparent? Can leadership forecast future performance reliably? These questions become central during the IPO process because institutional investors are responsible for managing billions of dollars in capital. Pension funds, hedge funds, mutual funds, insurance companies, and large asset managers do not simply invest based on excitement or optimism. They analyze financial structures carefully to determine whether a business deserves long-term shareholder investment.

This is why financial preparation must begin long before a company files for an IPO. Businesses that succeed in public markets typically spend years strengthening accounting systems, improving reporting accuracy, establishing internal controls, optimizing margins, and developing financial forecasting capabilities. Strong financial foundations create credibility, and credibility attracts investor confidence.

One of the first major areas companies must address is accounting standardization. Private companies sometimes operate with inconsistent accounting procedures, informal bookkeeping practices, or incomplete reporting structures. Public companies cannot function this way. Investors require financial statements prepared according to recognized accounting standards such as Generally Accepted Accounting Principles (GAAP) or International Financial Reporting Standards (IFRS), depending on the market and jurisdiction. Standardized accounting allows investors to compare companies consistently across industries and markets. Revenue recognition methods, expense reporting, asset valuation, liabilities, depreciation, and cash flow classifications must all follow established guidelines. Inaccurate or inconsistent accounting creates uncertainty, and uncertainty reduces investor confidence significantly.

Independent financial audits are another essential component of IPO preparation. Before going public, companies usually undergo multiple years of audited financial review performed by external accounting firms. Auditors examine company records, internal controls, financial statements, revenue documentation, tax filings, operational procedures, and compliance systems to verify accuracy and transparency.

The purpose of these audits is not simply regulatory compliance. Audits provide reassurance to investors that the company's financial reporting can be trusted. Public investors are placing capital into businesses they may never directly manage, so trust becomes a foundational element of public market participation.

Revenue quality also matters enormously during IPO evaluation. Investors analyze not only how much revenue a company generates, but also where that revenue comes from and how stable it is likely to remain. Companies with recurring revenue streams, subscription models, diversified customer bases, and long-term contracts are often viewed more favorably because their future income appears more predictable.

For example, a software company generating recurring monthly subscription income may receive a stronger valuation than a company dependent entirely on one-time sales transactions. Predictable cash flow reduces uncertainty, which investors generally reward through higher valuations.

Margin analysis becomes another critical financial focus. Public investors want to understand whether a company's profitability can improve as it scales. Gross margins, operating margins, net profit margins, and contribution margins all help investors evaluate business efficiency. High-growth companies operating at temporary losses may still attract investor interest if margins show long-term improvement potential and scalability.

This is particularly important in technology-driven businesses. Software companies often operate with high upfront development costs but relatively low incremental costs for serving additional customers. Once systems are built, scaling revenue can become highly efficient, creating the potential for expanding profit margins over time.

Cash flow management is equally important. Many companies appear successful on paper while quietly struggling with cash flow problems behind the scenes. Public investors analyze operating cash flow carefully because cash determines whether a business can sustain operations, fund expansion, manage debt obligations, and survive economic downturns.

A company with strong revenue growth but poor cash flow management may still face serious financial risk. Excessive spending, inefficient capital allocation, uncontrolled expansion, or poor receivables management can quickly create instability even within rapidly growing organizations.

Balance sheet strength also influences IPO readiness significantly. Investors review company assets, liabilities, debt levels, cash reserves, and working capital to determine financial health. Companies carrying excessive debt relative to earnings may face skepticism because high leverage increases financial vulnerability during economic downturns or market disruptions.

Conversely, companies with strong balance sheets and healthy liquidity positions often receive greater investor confidence because they appear better prepared to navigate uncertainty and continue investing in growth opportunities.

Forecasting capabilities become another major focus during IPO preparation. Public companies are expected to provide financial guidance and long-term strategic outlooks to investors. This requires sophisticated forecasting systems capable of projecting revenue, expenses, margins, growth trends, and operational performance with reasonable accuracy.

Investors lose confidence quickly when management repeatedly misses financial expectations. This is why companies preparing for IPOs invest heavily in financial planning systems, forecasting models, and performance analytics before entering public markets.

Internal controls represent another foundational component of financial readiness. Public companies must establish systems that reduce the risk of financial errors, fraud, reporting inconsistencies, or operational misconduct. Internal controls include approval procedures, reporting oversight, segregation of duties, cybersecurity protections, audit systems, compliance monitoring, and financial accountability structures.

Weak internal controls can become catastrophic in public markets. Financial scandals involving inaccurate reporting or executive misconduct have destroyed shareholder value repeatedly throughout history. Investors therefore place significant importance on governance and financial oversight systems.

Tax structure optimization is another important consideration before an IPO. Companies often work with financial advisors and tax specialists to ensure that corporate structures, ownership arrangements, and financial reporting strategies align efficiently with public market requirements. Poor tax planning can reduce profitability, create legal complications, or limit flexibility after public listing.

Equity structure also requires careful attention. Companies preparing for IPOs must evaluate stock ownership distribution, employee stock option plans, preferred shareholder rights, dilution exposure, and voting structures. Public investors generally prefer transparent equity structures without excessive complexity or unresolved ownership disputes.

The relationship between growth and profitability becomes a major strategic discussion during IPO preparation as well. Some companies prioritize aggressive expansion even at temporary losses because they believe capturing market share quickly creates long-term competitive advantages. Others emphasize profitability earlier to demonstrate operational discipline.

Public investors evaluate these strategies differently depending on industry conditions, market trends, and company positioning. High-growth industries may tolerate temporary losses more easily if long-term scalability appears strong. Mature industries often place greater emphasis on stable profitability and cash flow generation. Another critical financial concept involves unit economics. Investors want to understand whether individual customer relationships are financially sustainable. Customer acquisition costs, lifetime customer value, retention rates, churn levels, and contribution margins help investors evaluate whether the company can scale profitably over time.

A company may generate impressive overall revenue growth while still operating inefficiently at the customer level. Weak unit economics eventually create sustainability concerns, especially once public markets begin demanding long-term profitability visibility.

Financial storytelling also becomes increasingly important during the IPO process. Numbers alone rarely create investor enthusiasm. Leadership teams must explain how financial performance connects to larger strategic opportunities, industry trends, competitive advantages, and future growth potential.

For example, investors may tolerate temporary losses if leadership demonstrates a credible strategy for achieving future profitability through scale expansion, market dominance, or operational leverage. Effective financial communication therefore becomes a major skill for public company executives. Investor confidence depends heavily on predictability. Public markets reward companies capable of delivering consistent performance and reliable guidance. Businesses with erratic financial patterns, unpredictable earnings swings, or unstable operational performance often experience higher stock volatility and weaker investor support.

This is why many companies slow expansion intentionally before IPOs in order to stabilize operations and improve predictability. Sustainable growth often matters more to institutional investors than uncontrolled expansion.

Economic conditions also influence financial preparation strategies. During periods of low interest rates and strong investor optimism, public markets may tolerate higher valuations and temporary losses more easily. During uncertain economic environments, investors usually become more conservative and prioritize profitability, cash flow strength, and balance sheet stability.

Technology has dramatically improved financial management capabilities in recent decades. Modern companies now utilize advanced analytics platforms, artificial intelligence forecasting tools, automated reporting systems, and real-time financial dashboards to improve operational visibility and decision-making accuracy. These tools help companies strengthen financial discipline before entering public markets. Still, no software system can replace leadership accountability. Public investors ultimately evaluate whether management teams possess the discipline, transparency, and strategic thinking necessary to allocate shareholder capital responsibly. Financial preparation therefore extends beyond spreadsheets and reports. It reflects the overall maturity of the organization itself.

One of the most dangerous mistakes companies make before IPOs is focusing exclusively on valuation instead of sustainability. Some businesses attempt to maximize short-term growth metrics aggressively without building operational stability underneath the surface. While this approach may temporarily increase excitement, public markets eventually expose financial weaknesses.

Sustainable public companies are built on durable financial foundations. They understand cash flow management, maintain reporting transparency, allocate capital strategically, forecast realistically, and prioritize long-term operational strength alongside growth.

Preparing financially for an IPO also forces companies to become more disciplined businesses overall. Financial reporting improves decision-making. Internal controls reduce operational risk. Forecasting systems strengthen planning capabilities. Governance structures improve accountability. Even companies that ultimately choose not to go public often emerge stronger after implementing IPO-level financial standards.

Ultimately, public investors are not simply investing in products, technology, or branding. They are investing in a financial machine capable of generating long-term shareholder value consistently. The stronger the financial foundation beneath the company, the stronger the investor confidence surrounding the IPO.

The journey into public markets begins with numbers, discipline, transparency, and trust. Companies that build strong financial foundations position themselves not only for successful IPOs but also for sustainable long-term growth within the demanding environment of public capital markets.

The Numbers Behind the Dream: How NovaCore Nearly Lost Its IPO

When Ethan Walker founded NovaCore Analytics, he believed technology could revolutionize healthcare forecasting forever. The company developed artificial intelligence systems capable of predicting patient admission trends, resource shortages, and hospital operational risks before they occurred. The technology gained attention quickly because hospitals constantly struggled with staffing inefficiencies, overcrowding, and rising operational costs.

At first, NovaCore operated like many ambitious startups. Ethan focused obsessively on product innovation and aggressive growth. Investors loved the company's vision. Venture capital funding arrived quickly, allowing NovaCore to expand across multiple hospital systems nationwide. Revenue climbed dramatically each year.

Within six years, financial media outlets began referring to NovaCore as one of the most promising healthcare AI companies in the country. Investment bankers approached Ethan regularly about pursuing an Initial Public Offering.

Analysts believed the company could achieve a multi-billion-dollar valuation due to strong industry demand for healthcare automation technologies.

Employees celebrated constantly as stock option valuations increased internally. Early investors anticipated enormous profits. Public market excitement surrounding artificial intelligence companies created even greater pressure to launch the IPO quickly.

But beneath the surface, NovaCore had serious financial weaknesses that few outsiders understood. The company's accounting systems remained fragmented because growth happened faster than operational development. Different departments tracked revenue inconsistently. Customer contracts varied widely in structure and payment timing. Expense forecasting lacked precision. Financial reporting procedures depended heavily on manual processes created during the startup years.

Ethan knew the systems needed improvement eventually, but he believed rapid expansion mattered more in the short term.

"We'll clean everything up before the IPO," he told executives repeatedly.

As IPO preparation officially began, outside auditors arrived to review the company's financial records.

Problems appeared immediately.

Revenue recognition practices varied between departments. Some long-term customer contracts had been recorded inconsistently. Deferred revenue calculations contained errors. Certain operational expenses had been categorized improperly across multiple reporting periods.

The auditors were not accusing NovaCore of fraud. The business itself remained legitimate and highly innovative. But the financial systems lacked the structure and discipline required for public market standards.

The situation became even more stressful when investment bankers warned that institutional investors would examine financial transparency aggressively during roadshow presentations.

"If investors lose confidence in the reporting," one banker explained carefully, "valuation could collapse regardless of growth potential."

For the first time since founding the company, Ethan realized that innovation alone would not carry NovaCore into public markets successfully.

The next several months became some of the most difficult in company history.

NovaCore hired an experienced Chief Financial Officer named Rebecca Chen who previously helped lead two technology companies through successful IPOs. Rebecca immediately identified major weaknesses within the organization.

Financial forecasting lacked consistency. Internal controls were underdeveloped. Reporting systems could not scale efficiently. Operational departments communicated poorly regarding financial data.

Rebecca introduced strict new processes that frustrated many employees initially. Financial reporting became standardized. Expense approvals required additional oversight. Revenue recognition rules became far more disciplined. Forecasting models were rebuilt from scratch.

Some executives complained that the new systems slowed operations.

Rebecca disagreed completely.

"Public companies don't survive on excitement," she told the leadership team firmly. "They survive on trust."

Meanwhile, external pressure intensified. Competitors accelerated their own expansion efforts. Investors questioned why the IPO timeline kept getting delayed. Financial media began speculating about internal problems at NovaCore.

Ethan felt overwhelmed constantly. For years, he built the company around speed, innovation, and aggressive growth. Now he realized the business needed something equally important.

Financial maturity.

One evening, Ethan and Rebecca stayed late reviewing revised financial projections.

“We grew too fast,” Ethan admitted quietly. Rebecca shook her head.

“No,” she replied. “You grew exactly as a startup should grow. But now you’re becoming a public company. That requires a completely different level of discipline.”

Over the following year, NovaCore transformed internally.

Automated reporting systems replaced outdated manual processes. Financial dashboards provided real-time operational visibility. Internal audit systems strengthened compliance oversight. Revenue forecasting improved dramatically. Customer contracts became standardized. Expense controls tightened significantly.

Most importantly, the leadership team learned how to operate with greater financial accountability.

The transformation was painful but powerful.

When NovaCore finally resumed IPO preparation, the difference became obvious immediately. Auditors praised the company's improved reporting systems. Institutional investors responded positively to the stronger financial transparency. Analysts noted that operational discipline had improved substantially.

During the investor roadshow, Ethan noticed a major shift in conversations. Previously, investors focused mostly on growth potential and artificial intelligence trends. Now they asked detailed questions about margins, customer retention, cash flow management, scalability efficiency, and long-term profitability strategy.

This time, NovaCore had strong answers.

The IPO launched successfully months later with strong institutional demand. The company achieved a high valuation, but more importantly, investors trusted the leadership team's financial discipline and operational transparency.

After the public listing, NovaCore continued growing steadily instead of collapsing under public market pressure like many overhyped technology companies.

Several years later, Ethan spoke at an entrepreneurship conference where a young founder asked him what mattered most before going public.

"Technology matters," Ethan said. "Vision matters. Growth matters. But public markets ultimately invest in trust. If your numbers are weak, your systems are weak, or your reporting lacks discipline, investors will eventually find out."

He paused briefly before continuing. "A public company isn't just a product or idea anymore. It becomes a financial institution responsible for protecting shareholder confidence every single quarter."

The audience remained silent as Ethan reflected on NovaCore's journey.

The company almost entered public markets too early. Excitement and valuation pressure nearly pushed leadership into a dangerous mistake. But by rebuilding the company's financial foundation before going public, NovaCore positioned itself for something far more valuable than temporary hype.

It positioned itself for long-term survival.

And in public markets, survival is what eventually creates legends.

Chapter 4

Selecting Investment Banks, Advisors, and the IPO Team

One of the most important decisions a company makes during the Initial Public Offering process is choosing the team responsible for guiding the business into public markets. No company completes an IPO alone. The process requires collaboration between investment banks, attorneys, accountants, auditors, financial advisors, investor relations specialists, regulatory consultants, and executive leadership teams working together strategically under intense timelines and public scrutiny. The quality of this team can significantly influence valuation, investor demand, market credibility, regulatory compliance, and the long-term success of the company after listing.

For many founders, choosing an IPO team is unfamiliar territory. Entrepreneurs may spend years building products, managing employees, raising private capital, and scaling operations without ever interacting deeply with Wall Street institutions or securities law firms. Yet once IPO preparation begins, these external advisors become some of the most influential participants in the company's future. Selecting the right partners therefore requires careful analysis, strategic thinking, and long-term alignment rather than simply choosing the largest or most recognizable firms available.

The center of the traditional IPO process is usually the lead investment bank, commonly referred to as the underwriter. Investment banks serve multiple critical functions during an IPO. They help determine company valuation, structure the offering, coordinate regulatory filings, market shares to institutional investors, organize roadshows, and facilitate the actual distribution of stock into public markets. Underwriters essentially act as intermediaries between the company and the investing public.

The reputation of the lead investment bank matters enormously because investor confidence is often influenced by the institutions supporting the offering. Well-respected investment banks bring credibility, relationships, research coverage, institutional investor access, and capital markets expertise that can strengthen the IPO process significantly. Institutional investors frequently evaluate which banks are underwriting an offering before deciding whether to participate.

However, choosing the right investment bank involves far more than prestige alone. Different banks specialize in different industries, company sizes, and market segments. A technology-focused investment bank may understand software and artificial intelligence businesses deeply but possess limited expertise in manufacturing or healthcare. Some banks specialize in high-growth startups, while others focus more heavily on mature corporations with stable cash flow profiles.

Companies therefore need to evaluate whether an investment bank truly understands the business model, industry dynamics, growth strategy, and investor audience relevant to the company's specific market position. Alignment matters because underwriters help shape how the company is presented to institutional investors during the IPO process.

Another important consideration involves the level of attention the company will receive from the bank itself. Large investment banks may prioritize billion-dollar offerings involving massive corporate clients, while smaller companies risk becoming lower-priority accounts within the organization. Mid-sized or specialized banks sometimes provide more focused attention and stronger alignment for emerging growth companies seeking meaningful strategic guidance.

Investment banks also influence IPO pricing strategy. During the offering process, underwriters work closely with institutional investors to determine market demand and establish the appropriate share price range. Pricing too aggressively can reduce aftermarket stock performance and damage investor confidence. Pricing too conservatively may leave significant capital on the table that could have benefited the company.

Balancing these interests requires experience, market knowledge, and investor insight. Strong underwriters understand how to position offerings strategically to maximize both capital raising and long-term shareholder support.

In many IPOs, multiple investment banks participate together as underwriting syndicates. The lead underwriter coordinates the overall process while additional banks help distribute shares, provide investor relationships, and expand market reach. Syndicate structures allow companies to access broader institutional networks while diversifying underwriting support across multiple financial institutions.

Beyond investment banks, securities attorneys play another essential role during IPO preparation. Public offerings involve highly regulated legal frameworks requiring extensive compliance with securities laws, disclosure standards, corporate governance requirements, and regulatory filings. Securities attorneys help prepare registration documents, review disclosures, structure offering agreements, manage regulatory communication, and reduce legal exposure throughout the process. Legal teams also help companies evaluate risk factors requiring disclosure to investors. Public companies must provide detailed information about operational risks, competitive threats, market uncertainties, litigation exposure, financial vulnerabilities, and strategic challenges that could influence shareholder outcomes. Failing to disclose material risks accurately can create serious legal and financial consequences after listing.

Accounting firms and auditors represent another foundational part of the IPO team. Public investors rely heavily on audited financial statements when evaluating companies. Independent accounting firms verify reporting accuracy, review internal controls, examine financial procedures, and ensure compliance with accounting standards. Credible audit firms strengthen investor confidence because they provide external validation of the company's financial condition.

Investor relations specialists also become increasingly important during IPO preparation. Public companies must communicate effectively with institutional investors, analysts, shareholders, financial media, and market participants. Investor relations professionals help craft messaging strategies, coordinate investor presentations, prepare executive communication materials, and manage market perception before and after listing. Communication becomes especially important during roadshows, where executives present the company's story directly to institutional investors. Investors evaluate not only the financial opportunity itself but also leadership credibility, communication clarity, strategic vision, and executive confidence. Strong investor relations preparation helps executives deliver consistent, persuasive messaging under pressure.

Public relations advisors often support the IPO process as well. Media coverage surrounding public offerings can influence market perception significantly. Positive coverage may increase visibility and investor interest, while negative publicity or poorly managed communication can damage confidence rapidly. Strategic public relations planning helps companies control narratives, strengthen branding, and respond effectively to media scrutiny.

Another important advisor category includes governance consultants and compliance specialists. Public companies operate within strict governance frameworks involving board independence, executive accountability, compliance procedures, internal controls, and shareholder protections. Governance advisors help companies strengthen operational structures before entering public markets.

This often includes forming independent board committees, implementing ethical reporting systems, establishing compliance procedures, and improving executive oversight. Governance quality influences investor trust heavily because weak oversight structures increase perceived operational risk.

Selecting board members becomes another major strategic decision during IPO preparation. Public company boards are expected to include individuals with industry expertise, financial knowledge, operational experience, and governance credibility. Investors frequently evaluate board composition carefully because boards influence long-term strategic direction and executive accountability.

Companies often recruit experienced executives from other public corporations to strengthen board credibility before IPOs. Independent directors with strong reputations can improve investor confidence substantially by demonstrating that the company values governance discipline and shareholder accountability.

Internal leadership alignment also matters significantly during advisor selection. IPO preparation places enormous stress on executive teams because the process requires intense coordination across departments, advisors, legal teams, auditors, and investors simultaneously. Leadership teams must operate cohesively under pressure while maintaining day-to-day business performance. Strong communication between internal executives and external advisors becomes essential. Misalignment, confusion, or poor coordination can delay filings, create disclosure errors, weaken investor presentations, or damage offering execution.

Another major consideration involves advisor incentives. Investment banks earn underwriting fees based on offering size, while legal and accounting firms generate substantial revenue from IPO preparation services. Companies therefore need advisors who prioritize long-term success rather than simply maximizing transaction volume or short-term fees.

Experienced founders often evaluate whether advisors genuinely believe in the company's long-term vision or merely view the IPO as another transaction. The best advisors usually act as strategic partners invested in helping the company succeed after listing, not just during the offering itself.

Chemistry and trust also matter more than many founders initially realize. IPO preparation can become emotionally exhausting and operationally overwhelming. Executives spend months under pressure managing deadlines, investor expectations, regulatory reviews, and public scrutiny. Working with advisors who communicate clearly, remain calm under pressure, and maintain strategic focus can significantly improve the process. Companies should also evaluate how investment banks intend to support the business after the IPO. Research analyst coverage, institutional investor relationships, secondary offerings, follow-on capital raises, acquisition financing, and long-term market support all become important after listing. Some underwriters remain highly engaged post-IPO, while others shift focus quickly to newer transactions.

The due diligence process conducted by advisors can also reveal important internal weaknesses before entering public markets. Strong advisors challenge assumptions aggressively, identify operational risks, improve disclosures, strengthen governance, and force leadership teams to prepare more thoroughly. While this process can feel uncomfortable, it often strengthens the company significantly before public listing.

Industry specialization increasingly influences advisor selection as well. Technology IPOs differ substantially from healthcare, biotechnology, manufacturing, energy, or financial services offerings. Industry-specific knowledge helps advisors position companies more effectively because they understand sector-specific metrics, investor expectations, valuation frameworks, and regulatory considerations.

Global expansion has also increased the complexity of IPO advisory relationships. Many companies now operate internationally before going public, requiring expertise in cross-border regulations, international accounting standards, foreign market disclosures, currency risks, and multinational investor communication strategies.

Another challenge companies face is balancing advisor opinions. Investment banks may recommend aggressive growth positioning to maximize investor excitement, while attorneys emphasize risk disclosures and caution. Auditors prioritize reporting accuracy and compliance, while investor relations teams focus on market perception and communication strategy.

Leadership teams must navigate these competing perspectives carefully. Successful IPO execution often depends on balancing optimism with realism, growth ambition with operational discipline, and investor enthusiasm with regulatory transparency.

Technology has also transformed the advisor landscape in modern capital markets. Data analytics, investor targeting systems, virtual roadshows, digital reporting tools, and real-time market analysis platforms now play significant roles during IPO preparation. Advisors capable of leveraging modern technology effectively may provide strategic advantages during offering execution.

Still, despite technological advancements, relationships remain central to the IPO process. Institutional investors trust underwriters with strong reputations. Regulators respect experienced legal teams. Markets respond positively to credible leadership. Human trust continues driving capital allocation decisions at every level of public markets.

Selecting the IPO team is therefore not simply about hiring service providers. It is about building a network of strategic partners capable of guiding the company through one of the most important transitions in its history. The right advisors can strengthen investor confidence, improve execution quality, reduce operational risk, and position the company for long-term public market success.

The companies that navigate IPOs most successfully usually surround themselves with experienced, aligned, disciplined advisors who understand both the technical and strategic realities of entering public markets. Strong teams create stronger offerings, and stronger offerings create stronger long-term foundations for life as a public company.

The Team That Took VertexOne Public

When Maya Bennett first met with the investment bankers from New York, she felt completely out of place.

The conference room overlooking Manhattan was filled with polished executives in expensive suits speaking rapidly about valuation multiples, institutional demand curves, underwriting spreads, and market timing strategies. Maya had spent the last decade building VertexOne Robotics from a small industrial automation startup into a rapidly growing robotics software company serving manufacturing facilities across the country.

She understood technology.

She understood engineering.

She understood operations.

But Wall Street was an entirely different world.

VertexOne had experienced explosive growth over the previous four years. The company's robotics optimization systems dramatically improved manufacturing efficiency by reducing downtime and increasing production accuracy through machine-learning automation. Major manufacturing companies began integrating VertexOne systems into facilities nationwide.

Revenue climbed aggressively. Venture capital firms invested heavily. Financial media labeled VertexOne one of the fastest-growing industrial AI companies in America.

Now investors and board members wanted to pursue an Initial Public Offering. Maya understood the opportunity. Public markets could provide the capital needed to expand internationally, accelerate research and development, and acquire smaller robotics competitors. But she also realized something equally important.

The success of the IPO would depend heavily on the people guiding the process.

The first investment bank presentation impressed many board members immediately. The bank was globally recognized and had led several major technology IPOs recently. Their pitch deck included billion-dollar valuation projections and aggressive market expansion forecasts.

But something felt wrong to Maya.

Throughout the presentation, the bankers barely discussed VertexOne's actual technology, customer relationships, or long-term strategy. Instead, they focused almost entirely on maximizing short-term IPO excitement and media attention.

After the meeting ended, Maya turned to her Chief Operating Officer quietly.

"They understand the market," she said carefully, "but I'm not sure they understand our company."

Over the next several weeks, VertexOne interviewed multiple investment banks, law firms, auditors, and investor relations advisors.

Some firms emphasized prestige and market visibility. Others highlighted industry expertise and long-term strategic support. Maya quickly realized that choosing advisors resembled hiring executives more than hiring vendors.

Every advisor would influence how investors perceived the company.

Eventually, Maya narrowed the lead underwriting candidates to two investment banks.

The first was one of the largest and most recognizable firms on Wall Street. Their reputation alone could attract massive investor attention. However, VertexOne would represent a relatively small client within their enormous organization.

The second bank was smaller but specialized heavily in industrial technology and robotics companies. Their executives understood manufacturing systems deeply and maintained strong relationships with institutional investors focused specifically on industrial automation.

During the final selection meeting, Maya asked both banks the same question. “What happens after the IPO?”

The first bank discussed future stock offerings, analyst coverage, and media exposure.

The second bank discussed long-term operational execution, investor communication discipline, and building credibility quarter after quarter as a public company.

That answer changed everything.

Maya selected the smaller specialized bank despite pressure from several investors who preferred the larger institution.

“You’re choosing expertise over prestige,” one board member said skeptically.

“No,” Maya replied calmly. “I’m choosing alignment.”

The decision proved critical almost immediately.

The underwriting team challenged VertexOne aggressively during due diligence. They identified weaknesses in reporting systems, questioned customer concentration risks, and pushed leadership to strengthen operational forecasting before entering public markets.

At first, several executives found the process frustrating.

“Why are they making everything harder?” the sales director complained after one particularly difficult strategy meeting.

“They’re preparing us for public investors,” Maya answered. “If we can’t answer difficult questions internally, we won’t survive public scrutiny externally.”

Meanwhile, the legal team uncovered several compliance vulnerabilities related to international licensing agreements that required restructuring before the IPO. The accounting firm identified inconsistencies in historical revenue reporting procedures that needed correction.

The process became exhausting.

Executives worked late into the night revising disclosures, strengthening internal controls, improving governance systems, and rebuilding operational reporting frameworks. Some employees questioned whether the IPO was worth the stress.

But slowly, the company became stronger.

The board expanded with experienced independent directors

from public manufacturing and technology firms. Investor relations specialists coached executives extensively for institutional presentations. Public relations advisors prepared communication strategies for media coverage and analyst scrutiny. Most importantly, Maya began learning how differently public investors viewed companies compared to venture capital firms.

Private investors focused heavily on disruption and future growth potential. Public investors still valued growth, but they also demanded predictability, governance discipline, operational transparency, and execution consistency.

The IPO roadshow finally began nearly eighteen months after the initial advisor selection process started.

Maya traveled constantly alongside the underwriting team meeting institutional investors across New York, Boston, Chicago, San Francisco, and London. Every presentation required precision. Investors challenged assumptions aggressively.

“How sustainable are manufacturing margins during economic slowdowns?”

“What prevents competitors from replicating the technology?”

“How scalable is the implementation process globally?”

"What operational controls exist for cybersecurity risks?"

The advisors Maya selected prepared her for every question. One evening after a long day of investor meetings, Maya sat with the lead banker reviewing demand data from institutional investors.

"The market response is strong," he said. "Investors trust the story because they trust the preparation behind it."

Maya realized then that the IPO process was never just about selling shares.

It was about building credibility.

When VertexOne officially entered public markets, investor demand exceeded expectations significantly. The stock performed strongly after listing, but unlike many overhyped IPOs, the company maintained stability because operational systems and leadership preparation supported the valuation.

Months later, Maya attended a leadership conference where another founder asked her what mattered most during IPO preparation.

"The team," Maya answered immediately.

"Not just the executives inside your company. The bankers, attorneys, auditors, advisors, investor relations people, governance experts—everyone. Public markets are too complex to navigate alone."

She paused briefly before continuing.

"The wrong advisors can help you go public quickly. The right advisors help you survive after you get there."

Years later, VertexOne became one of the most respected industrial automation companies in global manufacturing. Analysts frequently praised the company's disciplined execution and operational consistency.

Looking back, Maya often believed the IPO succeeded long before the stock ever began trading publicly.

It succeeded the moment she stopped chasing prestige and started building the right team.

Because in public markets, the people surrounding a company often determine whether it becomes a temporary headline or a long-term institution.

Chapter 5

Preparing SEC Filings, Regulatory Compliance, and IPO Documentation

One of the most demanding and technically complex stages of the Initial Public Offering process involves preparing the regulatory filings and compliance documentation required for entry into public markets. While public attention often focuses on valuation, stock pricing, and investor excitement, the foundation of every traditional IPO is built upon disclosure, transparency, and regulatory accountability. Public markets function on trust, and regulators exist to ensure that investors receive accurate, complete, and fair information before making investment decisions.

For companies preparing to go public in the United States, the Securities and Exchange Commission (SEC) becomes one of the most important institutions involved in the IPO process. The SEC's primary responsibility is protecting investors and maintaining fair, orderly, and efficient markets. Any company seeking to offer shares publicly must comply with securities regulations and provide extensive disclosures regarding its operations, finances, leadership structure, risks, and business strategy. For many founders, the SEC filing process becomes their first experience operating within the strict regulatory framework governing public corporations. Private companies often enjoy flexibility regarding operational transparency because ownership remains limited to founders, private investors, and internal stakeholders. Public companies operate differently. Once shares are offered to the public, investors have the legal right to receive detailed information about the business they are investing in.

This requirement for transparency creates one of the defining differences between private and public companies. The IPO process effectively transforms the company from a relatively private organization into a highly visible institution operating under continuous disclosure obligations.

The most important filing document during the IPO process is typically the registration statement, commonly referred to as the Form S-1 in the United States. The S-1 filing represents a comprehensive overview of the company's business, financial condition, operations, leadership, risk factors, market opportunity, and offering structure. It serves as the primary document investors use to evaluate whether the company represents an attractive investment opportunity.

Preparing the S-1 is an enormous undertaking. Legal teams, accountants, auditors, executives, underwriters, and compliance specialists often spend months coordinating information, reviewing disclosures, verifying financial data, and refining language throughout the document. Every section must be accurate because misleading disclosures can create severe legal and financial consequences after the company becomes public.

One of the most heavily scrutinized sections of the S-1 involves financial statements. Companies must provide audited historical financial information covering multiple reporting periods. Investors analyze revenue trends, margins, expenses, liabilities, cash flow, debt levels, and operational performance carefully when evaluating IPO opportunities.

The financial sections also include management discussion and analysis, commonly referred to as MD&A. This section allows leadership to explain financial results, operational trends, strategic priorities, market conditions, and business outlook in greater detail. Investors rely heavily on management commentary because numbers alone rarely provide full context regarding company performance.

Risk factor disclosures represent another major component of IPO filings. Public companies must identify and disclose risks that could materially affect business performance, financial stability, operations, or shareholder value. These risks may include competition, cybersecurity threats, regulatory changes, customer concentration, economic downturns, supply chain disruptions, litigation exposure, technology dependence, intellectual property disputes, and leadership transitions.

Many founders initially dislike the risk disclosure process because it forces companies to describe vulnerabilities publicly. However, regulators require these disclosures because investors must understand both the opportunities and dangers associated with the investment.

Ironically, strong risk disclosure often improves credibility rather than damaging it. Investors understand that all businesses face challenges. Companies that communicate risks transparently are often viewed as more trustworthy than those attempting to minimize or hide potential problems.

Another important area involves corporate governance disclosures. Public investors want to understand how the company is managed, how executive decisions are supervised, and what protections exist for shareholders. IPO filings therefore include detailed information regarding board composition, executive compensation, shareholder rights, voting structures, governance committees, and ethical compliance systems.

Executive compensation becomes a particularly sensitive disclosure topic because public investors closely examine how leadership teams are paid. Excessive executive compensation packages, poorly structured incentives, or governance conflicts can attract shareholder criticism quickly after public listing.

Ownership disclosures also play a major role in IPO documentation. Investors want clarity regarding who controls the company, how shares are distributed, and how future dilution could affect shareholder value. IPO filings therefore identify major shareholders, founder ownership positions, institutional investors, preferred stock arrangements, and employee equity programs.

Use of proceeds disclosures represent another important section of IPO filings. Companies must explain how they intend to use the capital raised through the offering. Common uses include expansion initiatives, debt reduction, acquisitions, infrastructure investment, product development, research and development, international growth, or general corporate purposes.

Investors evaluate these plans carefully because capital allocation strategy significantly influences long-term shareholder value. Companies that communicate disciplined and strategic use of IPO proceeds often attract stronger institutional support. Regulatory review by the SEC can become highly detailed and time-consuming. After reviewing the initial filing, regulators frequently issue comment letters requesting clarification, additional disclosures, revisions, or expanded explanations regarding various aspects of the business. Companies may go through multiple rounds of revisions before the SEC allows the registration statement to move forward.

This review process helps ensure that investors receive complete and accurate information before shares become publicly tradable. While many founders view regulatory review as frustrating, it ultimately strengthens disclosure quality and market integrity.

Confidential filing options have become increasingly common in modern IPO markets. Some companies initially submit draft registration statements confidentially before making them public later in the process. This allows businesses to address regulatory feedback privately before public disclosure occurs, reducing reputational risk if delays or revisions become necessary.

Compliance preparation extends far beyond the IPO itself. Public companies must establish ongoing reporting systems capable of meeting quarterly and annual filing obligations after listing. This includes preparing Forms 10-Q, 10-K, 8-K disclosures, earnings reports, proxy statements, and shareholder communications consistently and accurately.

The Sarbanes-Oxley Act also introduced significant compliance obligations for public companies following major corporate accounting scandals in the early 2000s. These regulations strengthened internal control requirements, executive accountability standards, audit oversight procedures, and financial certification obligations.

Under Sarbanes-Oxley requirements, executives must certify the accuracy of financial statements personally. Companies must also establish internal controls designed to reduce the risk of financial errors or misconduct. Compliance failures can result in severe penalties, legal exposure, reputational damage, and shareholder lawsuits.

Cybersecurity disclosure has become another increasingly important area of regulatory focus. As technology dependence grows across industries, regulators and investors expect companies to identify cybersecurity risks, data protection vulnerabilities, and digital infrastructure threats more transparently. Public companies experiencing significant cyber incidents may face immediate disclosure obligations depending on materiality.

Environmental, social, and governance considerations, commonly known as ESG factors, have also gained importance in modern IPO filings. Institutional investors increasingly evaluate sustainability practices, labor policies, environmental impact, diversity initiatives, governance structures, and ethical standards when assessing long-term investment opportunities.

Globalization has further increased regulatory complexity for many IPO candidates. Companies operating internationally may face foreign regulatory obligations, international accounting requirements, cross-border compliance risks, and multinational disclosure considerations. Managing these obligations requires extensive coordination between legal, financial, and compliance teams.

The documentation process itself forces companies to examine their operations in extraordinary detail. Weaknesses that may remain unnoticed in private environments often become visible during IPO preparation. Inconsistent contracts, unclear ownership rights, operational gaps, reporting deficiencies, governance weaknesses, and unresolved legal issues may all surface during the filing process.

This is one reason strong legal and compliance teams are so essential during IPO preparation. Experienced advisors help companies identify vulnerabilities early and resolve issues before they become public market problems.

Communication discipline becomes increasingly important once regulatory filings begin. Public companies and IPO candidates must follow strict communication guidelines regarding forward-looking statements, investor discussions, financial projections, and media interactions. Selective disclosure or misleading public communication can create legal exposure and regulatory concerns.

The concept of the "quiet period" also plays an important role during IPO preparation. During certain stages of the process, companies and executives face restrictions regarding promotional communication intended to influence investor demand improperly. Compliance with these communication rules helps preserve fair market conditions.

For founders, the SEC filing process can feel emotionally difficult because it exposes large portions of the business publicly for the first time. Competitors gain access to operational details. Financial performance becomes transparent. Risk disclosures become visible to the market. Leadership compensation and governance structures become public information.

However, transparency is one of the foundations of public market trust. Investors are willing to commit capital because disclosure standards create accountability. Public markets function efficiently only when investors receive reliable information enabling informed decision-making.

Companies that approach compliance strategically often emerge stronger from the process itself. Improved reporting systems, stronger governance structures, enhanced operational discipline, and increased accountability frequently improve organizational quality long before the IPO occurs.

Ultimately, regulatory compliance is not simply a legal requirement. It is part of building credibility with investors, regulators, analysts, and the market as a whole. Strong disclosure practices signal professionalism, maturity, transparency, and leadership confidence.

Successful public companies understand that trust is one of the most valuable assets in capital markets. Accurate filings, disciplined compliance, and transparent communication help create that trust. And in public markets, trust often determines whether investors remain supportive during both strong and difficult periods.

The IPO filing process may appear administrative on the surface, but in reality, it represents one of the most important transitions in the company's evolution. It is the moment when a private business formally prepares to become accountable not only to founders and investors, but to the public itself.

The Filing That Nearly Destroyed Horizon BioSystems

When Horizon BioSystems first announced plans to pursue an Initial Public Offering, the biotechnology industry reacted with excitement immediately.

The company had developed a groundbreaking artificial intelligence platform capable of accelerating drug discovery timelines dramatically. Pharmaceutical companies partnering with Horizon reduced early-stage research costs substantially while improving predictive accuracy for clinical trial candidates.

Investors believed the technology could transform the future of biotech development.

Founded by Dr. Elena Morris, Horizon BioSystems grew from a university research project into one of the most promising biotechnology companies in the country within less than eight years. Venture capital firms invested aggressively. Strategic pharmaceutical partnerships expanded rapidly. Financial media outlets described Horizon as a future multi-billion-dollar company.

By the time investment banks began discussing IPO valuations, enthusiasm surrounding the company seemed unstoppable.

But Elena quickly discovered that excitement alone meant nothing once the SEC filing process began.

The company's legal team assembled in a large conference room for the first major S-1 drafting session. Attorneys, auditors, underwriters, accountants, executives, and compliance advisors filled the room with stacks of documents covering nearly every aspect of Horizon's operations.

Elena initially believed the process would be straightforward.

She was wrong.

The attorneys immediately began asking difficult questions.

"Have all intellectual property rights been fully documented?"

"Are there unresolved licensing agreements connected to university research partnerships?"

"Do all employee stock option grants comply with current reporting requirements?"

"Are all clinical research disclosures complete?"

The deeper the team investigated, the more problems emerged.

Several early-stage licensing agreements lacked proper documentation. Certain research partnerships involved complicated intellectual property sharing arrangements. Internal reporting systems used different methodologies across departments. Some operational risks had never been formally documented.

None of these issues were catastrophic individually. But together, they created serious complications for the IPO filing process.

The investment bankers became increasingly concerned.

"If these disclosures aren't handled properly," one advisor warned, "investor confidence could weaken significantly."

Elena felt overwhelmed.

For years, she focused almost entirely on scientific innovation and company growth. Compliance systems, legal structures, and governance frameworks always seemed secondary compared to product development and research breakthroughs.

Now every operational detail mattered.

The SEC filing process forced Horizon BioSystems to examine itself with microscopic precision.

Weeks turned into months as attorneys revised disclosure language repeatedly. Auditors reviewed historical financial records in extreme detail. Compliance specialists rebuilt internal governance systems. Executives rewrote operational reporting procedures.

The risk disclosure section became particularly difficult.

The legal team insisted the company disclose extensive risks related to clinical trial uncertainty, pharmaceutical regulation, intellectual property disputes, cybersecurity exposure, and competitive biotech innovation.

Elena worried the disclosures would scare investors away.

One evening after another exhausting review session, she confronted the company's lead securities attorney.

"If we describe every possible risk," she asked, "won't investors lose confidence completely?"

The attorney shook his head calmly.

"Serious investors already know risks exist," he explained. "The danger isn't disclosing risk. The danger is appearing dishonest or unprepared."

That conversation changed Elena's perspective completely.

Instead of resisting disclosure transparency, Horizon's leadership began embracing it. The company strengthened governance systems aggressively. Independent board members joined the organization. Compliance reporting improved significantly. Cybersecurity protections expanded. Financial controls became far more disciplined.

The process delayed the IPO timeline substantially.

Financial media began speculating about internal problems at Horizon. Competitors attempted to exploit the delays publicly. Some investors became impatient and pressured leadership to accelerate the process.

But Elena refused.

"If we enter public markets," she told the board firmly, "we do it correctly."

Months later, Horizon finally submitted its revised S-1 filing publicly.

Analysts and institutional investors examined the document closely.

To Elena's surprise, investor response remained overwhelmingly positive.

The transparency of the disclosures actually increased confidence rather than weakening it. Institutional investors praised the company's detailed risk analysis, governance improvements, operational discipline, and intellectual property protections.

One healthcare fund manager explained it simply during a roadshow meeting.

"We don't expect biotech companies to be risk-free," he said. "We expect leadership teams to understand the risks honestly."

The IPO eventually launched successfully with strong institutional participation and significant investor demand. Horizon BioSystems entered public markets with a strong valuation and substantial credibility.

Years later, Elena often reflected on how close the company came to rushing into public markets before fully preparing its compliance and disclosure systems.

At a biotechnology leadership conference, a founder once asked her what surprised her most about the IPO process.

"The filings," Elena answered immediately.

"Everyone focuses on valuation and stock pricing. But the filings force you to confront the truth about your company. Every weakness. Every risk. Every operational gap. It's uncomfortable because transparency always is."

She paused briefly before continuing. "But public trust is built through transparency. Investors don't expect perfection. They expect honesty, discipline, and accountability."

Over time, Horizon BioSystems became one of the most respected biotechnology AI companies in the healthcare industry. The company survived difficult clinical periods, market volatility, and competitive pressure because investor trust remained strong even during uncertainty.

Looking back, Elena realized the SEC filing process had done far more than prepare the company for an IPO.

It forced Horizon BioSystems to become a stronger institution.

Because public markets ultimately reward companies willing to face reality honestly long before investors are forced to discover it themselves.

Chapter 6

Valuation Strategy and Determining What Your Company Is Worth

One of the most important and emotionally charged aspects of the Initial Public Offering process is determining company valuation. Valuation influences how much capital a company can raise, how much ownership founders and early investors retain, how institutional investors perceive opportunity, and how the market reacts once trading begins publicly. For many entrepreneurs, valuation represents more than numbers on paper. It reflects years of sacrifice, innovation, risk-taking, and persistence. Yet despite the emotional significance attached to valuation, public markets evaluate companies according to financial realities, investor expectations, industry conditions, and future growth potential rather than personal attachment alone.

Understanding valuation is critical because the success of an IPO often depends on pricing strategy. A company priced too aggressively may struggle after listing if investors believe the valuation exceeds realistic future growth expectations. A company priced too conservatively may leave significant capital on the table and dilute existing shareholders unnecessarily. The challenge is finding a balance that supports both strong investor demand and sustainable long-term market performance.

Many private company founders initially misunderstand valuation because private market pricing and public market pricing can differ substantially. Venture capital investors often invest based on future disruption potential and long-term market opportunity. Public market investors still care about growth, but they also emphasize operational discipline, financial transparency, profitability pathways, competitive durability, and predictability. This shift in investor psychology becomes highly important during IPO preparation.

At its core, valuation represents the market's estimate of what a business is worth based on current performance and future expectations. Public investors evaluate not only historical results but also future revenue growth, margin expansion potential, market dominance opportunities, scalability, competitive advantages, leadership quality, and economic conditions.

One of the most common valuation methods involves comparing the company against similar publicly traded businesses. These comparable companies, often called "comps," provide reference points based on valuation multiples already accepted by the market. Analysts may compare revenue multiples, earnings multiples, EBITDA multiples, price-to-sales ratios, gross margin profiles, growth rates, and operational metrics to estimate appropriate valuation ranges.

For example, high-growth software companies often trade at significantly higher revenue multiples than traditional manufacturing firms because software businesses may scale more efficiently and generate stronger future margins. Industry dynamics therefore influence valuation heavily.

Growth rate is one of the most powerful drivers of valuation in modern public markets. Investors are often willing to pay premium multiples for businesses demonstrating rapid and sustainable expansion. However, growth alone is not enough. Investors also evaluate the quality of growth. Revenue generated through unsustainable discounts, excessive marketing expenses, weak customer retention, or low-margin operations may not justify premium valuations over time.

This is why recurring revenue models often attract strong investor enthusiasm. Subscription-based businesses, software-as-a-service companies, and recurring contract models create more predictable cash flow visibility. Predictability reduces uncertainty, and lower uncertainty generally increases valuation.

Profitability also plays a major role, although its importance varies depending on industry and market conditions. During periods of strong investor optimism, markets may reward high-growth companies even if they remain temporarily unprofitable. Investors may believe that capturing market share rapidly creates future profitability opportunities once the company achieves scale.

However, during periods of economic uncertainty or tighter capital markets, investors often shift focus toward profitability, cash flow discipline, and balance sheet strength. Valuation expectations therefore change constantly depending on broader market sentiment.

Margin structure influences valuation significantly as well. Investors want to understand whether the company can improve profitability as it scales. Businesses with strong gross margins and operational leverage often receive higher valuations because incremental revenue growth may eventually produce substantial earnings expansion.

Scalability represents another critical valuation factor. Companies capable of expanding globally without proportionally increasing expenses often attract premium market valuations. Technology businesses, digital platforms, marketplaces, and network-effect-driven companies frequently benefit from this dynamic because their infrastructure may support massive growth efficiently. Total addressable market, commonly referred to as TAM, also influences investor perception heavily. Investors evaluate how large the potential market opportunity could become over time. A company operating within a massive global industry may justify higher valuation multiples because future expansion potential appears greater.

Leadership credibility can influence valuation more than many founders initially realize. Investors place significant trust in executive teams when evaluating future growth assumptions. Experienced leadership with strong execution history often improves investor confidence and supports stronger valuation outcomes.

This is particularly true for founder-led companies. Public investors frequently analyze whether founders possess the discipline, strategic thinking, communication skills, and operational maturity necessary to lead public corporations successfully. Strong leadership can strengthen valuation because investors view capable management teams as critical drivers of future performance.

Timing also matters enormously during valuation discussions. Public market conditions fluctuate constantly based on economic trends, interest rates, geopolitical events, inflation expectations, investor sentiment, and industry momentum. During bullish markets, investors may support elevated valuations aggressively. During uncertain periods, valuation expectations often decline sharply even for strong companies.

Interest rates play a particularly important role because they influence investor appetite for growth-oriented businesses. Low interest rate environments tend to encourage investment into higher-growth assets, while higher rates often increase investor preference for stable profitability and cash flow generation.

One of the most dangerous mistakes companies make during IPO preparation is becoming emotionally attached to unrealistic valuation expectations. Founders who focus excessively on achieving the highest possible valuation sometimes ignore long-term market sustainability. Overpriced IPOs frequently struggle after listing because investor expectations become nearly impossible to satisfy.

A successful IPO is not simply one that launches at a high valuation. A successful IPO creates long-term investor confidence, stable trading performance, and sustainable access to public capital markets over time.

Institutional investors also analyze dilution carefully during valuation discussions. Issuing too many shares may reduce ownership percentages for founders and early investors significantly. However, raising insufficient capital may limit future growth opportunities. Balancing dilution and capital efficiency becomes an important strategic consideration.

Another important concept during valuation strategy is aftermarket performance. Investment banks often attempt to price IPOs in ways that allow positive early trading momentum after listing. Strong aftermarket performance creates positive publicity, investor enthusiasm, and market credibility. Poor aftermarket performance may damage company reputation and weaken future investor trust.

This is one reason underwriters sometimes encourage conservative pricing approaches even when market excitement appears strong. Leaving some upside potential for public investors may create healthier long-term relationships with institutional shareholders.

Roadshows become highly important during valuation determination because investor demand directly influences pricing outcomes. During roadshow presentations, institutional investors provide feedback regarding valuation expectations, growth assumptions, risk perceptions, and market interest levels. Underwriters use this information to refine pricing strategy before the IPO launches officially.

Investor psychology therefore plays a central role in valuation. Markets are driven not only by numbers but also by confidence, narratives, expectations, and future belief systems. Companies capable of communicating compelling growth stories supported by strong operational execution often achieve stronger valuation outcomes.

Brand positioning can also influence valuation significantly. Companies perceived as category leaders, disruptive innovators, or industry-defining platforms often attract stronger investor enthusiasm. Market leadership perception may support premium multiples beyond what financial statements alone would suggest.

Still, valuation discipline remains essential. Public markets eventually evaluate whether financial performance justifies pricing expectations. Companies unable to sustain growth or achieve operational execution after listing often experience significant stock declines regardless of initial excitement.

Private investors and venture capital firms also play important roles during valuation negotiations. Existing shareholders may pressure leadership teams to maximize IPO valuation in order to increase returns on earlier investments. However, overly aggressive pricing can damage long-term company performance if public investors lose confidence quickly after listing. Balancing these competing interests requires strong leadership and strategic thinking. The best IPO outcomes often involve realistic pricing aligned with sustainable operational execution rather than temporary hype-driven valuation spikes.

Market cycles have repeatedly demonstrated the dangers of irrational valuation behavior. During speculative periods, some companies achieve extreme valuations disconnected from financial fundamentals. Eventually, public markets tend to correct these imbalances when growth slows or investor sentiment changes.

This is why disciplined leadership teams focus on building durable businesses rather than chasing temporary market excitement. Sustainable valuation ultimately depends on consistent execution, operational quality, and long-term shareholder trust.

Financial forecasting becomes another major component of valuation strategy. Investors evaluate projected revenue growth, margin trends, customer expansion, operational scalability, and future profitability pathways when determining what they are willing to pay for shares. Accurate forecasting therefore strengthens credibility and supports stronger investor confidence.

Technology has also transformed valuation analysis in recent decades. Investors now evaluate companies using advanced data analytics, user engagement metrics, retention analysis, artificial intelligence forecasting models, and operational efficiency measurements. Public markets increasingly reward companies capable of demonstrating measurable scalability and performance transparency.

Yet despite increasingly sophisticated valuation methodologies, human psychology remains deeply influential. Fear, optimism, greed, uncertainty, confidence, and market narratives continue shaping public market behavior significantly. Successful companies understand how to balance financial fundamentals with investor psychology strategically.

Ultimately, valuation is not simply about assigning a number to a company. It represents the market's collective belief regarding the company's future potential. Strong valuations are earned through operational discipline, leadership quality, financial transparency, scalable systems, strategic positioning, and investor trust.

Companies that approach valuation strategically position themselves not only for successful IPO launches but also for stronger long-term public market performance. Sustainable wealth creation in public markets depends less on achieving the highest initial valuation and more on building businesses capable of growing into and beyond investor expectations over time.

The Billion-Dollar Debate at OrionCloud

When OrionCloud Technologies began preparing for its Initial Public Offering, excitement inside the company reached levels nobody had experienced before.

Founded by Lucas Grant and his longtime engineering partner Amelia Ross, OrionCloud built enterprise cybersecurity software designed to protect cloud infrastructure for large corporations. As remote work expanded globally and cyber threats increased dramatically, demand for OrionCloud's platform exploded.

The company's annual recurring revenue surged from twelve million dollars to over four hundred million dollars within five years. Major Fortune 500 corporations signed multi-year contracts rapidly. Venture capital firms invested aggressively. Financial media outlets began calling OrionCloud one of the most anticipated cybersecurity IPOs in the technology sector.

Inside headquarters, employees constantly discussed one topic.

Valuation.

Some analysts believed OrionCloud could launch publicly at a valuation exceeding twelve billion dollars. Others argued the company deserved even more due to explosive industry demand and high growth rates.

Lucas felt enormous pressure from investors and board members to maximize the IPO valuation aggressively.

"This market window may not stay open forever," one venture capital investor warned during a board meeting. "Cybersecurity companies are receiving premium multiples right now. We should push pricing as high as possible."

Several board members agreed immediately.

But Amelia remained skeptical.

Late one evening after another exhausting valuation meeting, Amelia sat with Lucas reviewing financial models quietly.

"I think we're becoming too focused on the number," she said carefully.

Lucas leaned back in frustration.

"Easy for you to say," he replied. "Everyone expects us to hit a massive valuation. Employees, investors, media—everyone."

Amelia looked directly at him.

"And what happens if we price too high and disappoint public investors six months later?"

The question stayed in Lucas's mind constantly afterward.

Over the following weeks, the underwriting banks conducted extensive investor meetings and valuation analysis. Public market comparables showed strong pricing potential, but investors also expressed concerns about slowing economic conditions and rising interest rates.

The company itself remained highly successful, but public markets were becoming more cautious.

Some executives wanted to emphasize growth aggressively during roadshow presentations. Others believed the company should highlight profitability pathways and operational discipline instead.

Tension inside the leadership team increased daily.

Meanwhile, employees grew obsessed with internal valuation rumors. Stock option calculations circulated constantly throughout the company. Social media discussions speculated wildly about how wealthy early employees might become after the IPO.

Lucas began realizing that valuation carried emotional pressure far beyond finance alone.

One afternoon, OrionCloud's lead investment banker presented revised pricing scenarios. "If we push aggressively," he explained, "the company could potentially launch near thirteen billion."

The room became silent.

"But?" Lucas asked.

The banker paused briefly.

"But public investors will expect near-perfect execution afterward. Any slowdown in growth, margin pressure, or operational weakness could create major volatility."

Amelia nodded immediately.

"What's the more sustainable range?" she asked.

The banker adjusted the projections.

"Closer to ten billion."

Several board members reacted negatively.

"That leaves billions on the table," one investor argued sharply.

"No," Amelia answered calmly. "It leaves room for trust."

The debate intensified over the next several days. Some investors believed conservative pricing would signal weakness. Others worried aggressive valuation could damage long-term market credibility if expectations became unrealistic.

Finally, Lucas made the decision.

OrionCloud would pursue disciplined pricing rather than maximum short-term valuation.

The choice disappointed several early investors initially, but the leadership team believed sustainable investor confidence mattered more than temporary headlines.

During the roadshow, institutional investors responded positively to the company's balanced approach. OrionCloud emphasized long-term cybersecurity demand, operational scalability, customer retention strength, and disciplined financial planning rather than exaggerated projections.

One institutional investor told Lucas privately after a presentation:

"Most IPO candidates try to convince us everything will be perfect forever. Your team actually sounds realistic."

That realism became a major advantage.

When OrionCloud finally entered public markets, investor demand remained extremely strong. The IPO launched successfully, and the stock traded upward steadily during the following months. More importantly, public investors maintained confidence because expectations aligned more realistically with operational performance.

As economic conditions became more volatile later that year, several aggressively priced technology IPOs collapsed under pressure after missing unrealistic growth expectations. OrionCloud, however, remained relatively stable because leadership prioritized sustainability over hype.

Years later, Lucas spoke at a technology founder summit where a young entrepreneur asked him how to maximize IPO valuation.

Lucas smiled slightly before answering.

"That's the wrong question."

The audience became quiet.

"The better question is how to build a company capable of earning investor trust for the next ten years."

He paused briefly before continuing.

"Anyone can chase a temporary valuation spike. But public markets eventually test whether the business underneath the number is real."

Looking back, Lucas realized the valuation debate at OrionCloud had never truly been about billions of dollars alone.

It was about discipline.

The company could have pursued maximum short-term pricing and celebrated a larger opening headline. Instead, leadership chose a valuation aligned with sustainable execution and long-term credibility.

That decision changed everything.

Because in public markets, the companies that survive longest are usually not the ones that promised the most.

They are the ones that delivered consistently after the excitement faded.

Chapter 7

The IPO Roadshow and Winning Institutional Investor Confidence

After years of preparation, financial restructuring, operational scaling, regulatory filings, and valuation discussions, one of the most important phases of the Initial Public Offering process finally begins: the IPO roadshow. The roadshow is where the company formally presents itself to institutional investors and attempts to secure the confidence necessary for a successful public market debut. For many executives and founders, this stage becomes one of the most intense, exhausting, and high-pressure experiences of their professional lives because the success of the offering often depends heavily on how effectively leadership communicates the company's story, strategy, financial opportunity, and long-term vision.

An IPO roadshow is far more than a marketing campaign. It is essentially a large-scale investor evaluation process where institutional investors analyze the company's business model, financial performance, leadership quality, competitive positioning, scalability, governance standards, and long-term growth potential. While investors review financial statements and regulatory filings carefully, many investment decisions are ultimately influenced by confidence in management itself. Investors want to believe not only in the company's numbers, but also in the people responsible for executing the business strategy after the company becomes public.

The primary participants in roadshows are institutional investors such as mutual funds, hedge funds, pension funds, insurance companies, sovereign wealth funds, family offices, and asset management firms. These institutions manage enormous pools of capital and often become major shareholders in newly public companies. Winning their support is critical because institutional investors can provide long-term shareholder stability, strong market credibility, and sustained trading demand after the IPO launches.

Roadshows are usually coordinated by the lead underwriters managing the IPO. Investment banks schedule meetings across major financial centers where executives present the company directly to institutional investors. In some cases, roadshows involve travel to cities such as New York, Boston, San Francisco, Chicago, London, Singapore, and other global investment hubs. In recent years, virtual roadshows have also become more common, allowing companies to present digitally to investors worldwide.

The structure of a roadshow presentation typically follows a carefully prepared format. Executives explain the company's history, mission, products or services, market opportunity, financial performance, competitive advantages, growth strategy, and long-term vision. Investors often ask detailed questions about margins, customer acquisition costs, scalability, regulatory risks, leadership decisions, market trends, competition, operational efficiency, and future profitability.

One of the most important realities founders learn during roadshows is that institutional investors evaluate companies differently than private investors. Venture capital firms may tolerate aggressive risk-taking, long development timelines, or uncertain profitability if disruption potential appears large enough. Public market investors still value growth, but they also emphasize predictability, governance, operational discipline, and execution consistency.

This shift in investor psychology requires leadership teams to adapt communication strategies carefully. Overpromising or presenting unrealistic projections can damage credibility quickly. Institutional investors have extensive experience analyzing businesses and often recognize exaggerated narratives immediately. Successful roadshows balance optimism with realism. Investors want ambitious growth potential, but they also want evidence that leadership understands operational risks and possesses disciplined execution strategies.

Leadership credibility becomes one of the most important factors influencing investor confidence during roadshows. Investors study executive behavior closely. They evaluate communication clarity, strategic understanding, confidence under pressure, financial knowledge, operational awareness, and honesty when discussing challenges or uncertainties.

Founders who built successful private companies may discover that public market communication requires entirely different skills. Public investors expect concise, disciplined, data-driven explanations supported by measurable evidence. Emotional enthusiasm alone rarely convinces sophisticated institutional investors.

Preparation therefore becomes essential before the roadshow begins. Executives often spend weeks practicing presentations, refining messaging, preparing for difficult investor questions, and improving communication discipline. Investor relations advisors and underwriters typically conduct mock interviews and presentation rehearsals to strengthen executive performance.

Consistency in messaging is extremely important throughout the roadshow process. Investors compare notes frequently. Contradictory statements, unclear explanations, or inconsistent growth narratives can weaken confidence quickly. Leadership teams must communicate unified strategic visions supported by accurate financial and operational details.

The company's growth story plays a major role during investor presentations. Investors want to understand not only what the company has achieved, but also what future opportunities exist. Leadership teams must explain market size, industry trends, competitive positioning, expansion opportunities, customer demand drivers, and scalability potential convincingly.

However, investors also examine whether the growth story is realistic. Companies operating in highly competitive industries must demonstrate clear differentiation. Businesses dependent on temporary market trends may face skepticism. Investors analyze whether growth drivers appear durable or temporary.

Competitive advantage therefore becomes a central discussion topic during most roadshows. Investors ask why competitors cannot easily replicate the company's success. Strong answers may involve proprietary technology, network effects, intellectual property, brand positioning, operational efficiency, customer loyalty, distribution advantages, or regulatory barriers to entry.

Financial performance discussions also dominate investor meetings. Institutional investors examine revenue growth, margin trends, recurring income stability, customer retention, operating expenses, scalability efficiency, and profitability pathways carefully. Leadership teams must demonstrate not only strong historical performance but also realistic future financial planning.

Questions regarding risk management are equally common. Investors want to know how the company plans to navigate economic downturns, cybersecurity threats, regulatory changes, operational disruptions, competitive pressure, supply chain risks, or technological shifts. Leadership credibility often strengthens when executives acknowledge risks openly while explaining mitigation strategies clearly.

One major objective of the roadshow is building investor trust. Public market investing ultimately involves uncertainty because investors cannot predict the future perfectly. Institutional shareholders therefore place enormous importance on management integrity and transparency. Companies perceived as trustworthy often receive stronger long-term investor support even during difficult periods.

Roadshows also help underwriters assess investor demand levels. Institutional investors provide feedback regarding valuation expectations, share allocation interest, pricing sensitivity, and overall market enthusiasm. Underwriters use this information to refine final IPO pricing strategies before the company officially enters public markets.

Book-building is another important process occurring simultaneously during the roadshow. Underwriters collect indications of interest from institutional investors regarding how many shares they may purchase at different pricing levels. Strong demand may support higher pricing or increased offering size. Weak demand may force pricing adjustments or strategic reconsideration.

The emotional intensity of roadshows can become overwhelming for leadership teams. Executives may conduct multiple presentations daily while traveling continuously under extreme pressure. Every meeting matters because institutional investor participation influences both IPO success and aftermarket trading stability.

Founders often experience emotional conflict during this process. Many entrepreneurs built their companies around innovation, product development, and customer relationships rather than financial presentations and shareholder communication. Yet roadshows force founders into highly visible public leadership roles where communication skill becomes just as important as operational capability. Media attention also increases significantly during roadshows. Financial journalists analyze investor reactions, valuation rumors, market sentiment, and leadership interviews closely. Public perception can influence investor psychology rapidly, especially during highly anticipated IPOs.

Another important factor influencing roadshow success is timing relative to broader market conditions. Even strong companies may struggle to generate investor enthusiasm during periods of economic uncertainty, market volatility, inflation concerns, geopolitical instability, or declining investor confidence. Conversely, bullish markets often create stronger demand for growth-oriented IPO opportunities.

Institutional investors also compare IPO candidates against existing public alternatives constantly. Investors evaluate whether purchasing newly issued shares offers more attractive opportunities than investing in already-public competitors. Companies therefore need compelling differentiation and strategic positioning to justify investor participation.

Some roadshows succeed because leadership teams inspire confidence immediately. Others struggle because executives appear unprepared, unrealistic, defensive, or disconnected from operational realities. Investors often remember how leadership behaves under pressure more than individual presentation slides or financial charts. Authenticity can become a major advantage during roadshows. Investors frequently meet leadership teams presenting polished but unrealistic narratives. Executives capable of communicating honestly, strategically, and confidently while acknowledging challenges often stand out positively.

Roadshows also reveal whether the company is culturally prepared for public markets. Public companies operate under constant scrutiny. Earnings calls, analyst questions, shareholder meetings, and media interviews continue long after the IPO itself. Leadership teams unable to communicate effectively with investors may struggle significantly after listing.

Another major challenge involves balancing long-term vision with short-term expectations. Public investors want evidence of future growth potential, but they also monitor quarterly performance closely. Leadership teams must communicate ambitious long-term strategies without creating unrealistic near-term expectations that could damage credibility later.

Technology has transformed roadshows in recent years as well.

Virtual investor meetings, digital presentation systems, data analytics platforms, and online institutional communication tools have increased efficiency and expanded global investor access. However, personal relationships and executive credibility remain deeply important despite technological advancements.

The strongest roadshows often create momentum extending beyond the IPO itself. Investors who develop confidence in management may continue supporting the company through future capital raises, acquisitions, expansion initiatives, or market volatility. Long-term investor relationships therefore begin forming during the roadshow process.

Ultimately, roadshows are not simply about selling shares. They are about introducing the company to the public investment community and establishing the foundation for future shareholder relationships. Strong roadshows create trust, credibility, and investor alignment capable of supporting long-term public market success.

Companies that prepare thoroughly, communicate strategically, and present realistic yet compelling visions often position themselves for stronger investor support both during and after the IPO. In public markets, investor confidence is one of the most valuable assets a company can possess, and the roadshow is where that confidence begins to form.

The Two Weeks That Changed NexaGrid Forever

When NexaGrid Energy Solutions officially began its IPO roadshow, CEO Aaron Delgado had not slept properly in nearly a month.

The company had spent years preparing for this moment.

Founded during the early expansion of renewable infrastructure technologies, NexaGrid developed advanced energy storage optimization software that helped utility companies balance renewable energy demand more efficiently. The company's artificial intelligence platform improved battery storage performance, reduced energy waste, and stabilized grid management for solar and wind power systems.

As governments and corporations accelerated renewable energy investments worldwide, NexaGrid's growth exploded.

Annual revenue tripled within three years. Strategic partnerships expanded internationally. Major institutional investors pushed aggressively for the company to pursue a public offering while market enthusiasm for clean energy technology remained strong.

Now the future of the IPO depended heavily on one thing. Investor confidence. Aaron sat quietly inside the company's private conference room early one morning reviewing presentation slides with the underwriting team before the first major investor meetings in New York.

"You need to simplify the scalability explanation," the lead banker advised. "Institutional investors understand technology, but they care most about execution and long-term profitability."

Aaron nodded, exhausted.

For years, he focused almost entirely on product development and operational growth. Public speaking never came naturally to him. Now he faced rooms filled with investors controlling billions of dollars in capital.

The first investor presentation began at 8:00 AM inside a Manhattan office tower overlooking the city skyline.

Aaron entered the room alongside the Chief Financial Officer and lead underwriters. Across the table sat portfolio managers, analysts, and institutional investors studying printed financial materials intensely before the presentation even started.

Aaron began explaining NexaGrid's technology platform, renewable infrastructure demand trends, customer growth, and international expansion opportunities.

The investors listened carefully but remained emotionally unreadable. Then the questions started.

"How defensible is the company's technology advantage?"

"What prevents larger competitors from entering the market aggressively?"

"How sensitive is future growth to government subsidy programs?"

"When does the company expect sustained profitability expansion?"

The intensity surprised Aaron immediately.

These were not startup investors chasing hype or speculative disruption narratives. These investors analyzed operational risk, financial durability, and long-term execution discipline with extreme precision.

By the end of the first day, Aaron had completed seven investor meetings across New York.

The following morning, the roadshow continued in Boston.

Then Chicago.

Then San Francisco.

Then London. Every day followed the same exhausting pattern. Investor meetings started early in the morning and often continued late into the evening. Aaron repeated the company's story constantly while adjusting explanations based on investor concerns and feedback.

Some meetings went exceptionally well.

Others felt brutal.

One hedge fund manager interrupted Aaron halfway through a presentation.

"Your growth projections assume near-perfect renewable infrastructure expansion," he said sharply. "What happens if the economy slows significantly?"

Aaron paused briefly.

Early in his entrepreneurial career, he would have reacted defensively. But months of preparation changed his perspective.

"There are absolutely risks," Aaron answered calmly. "Energy infrastructure cycles fluctuate. Competition will increase.

Regulation changes constantly. But global energy demand continues rising, and grid efficiency remains a long-term necessity regardless of short-term cycles."

The investor leaned back silently. After the meeting ended, the lead underwriter smiled slightly.

"That answer probably helped more than pretending risk doesn't exist."

As the roadshow continued, Aaron began understanding something deeply important about public markets.

Institutional investors were not looking for perfection.

They were looking for leadership teams capable of navigating uncertainty intelligently.

Investor feedback also influenced valuation discussions throughout the roadshow. Some institutions expressed strong enthusiasm about NexaGrid's market opportunity. Others pushed back against aggressive pricing expectations due to broader economic uncertainty.

Each evening, the underwriting team analyzed investor demand levels carefully through the book-building process. Interest remained strong overall, but pricing discipline became increasingly important.

Meanwhile, financial media coverage intensified daily.

Television analysts debated the company's valuation constantly. Online investors speculated aggressively about future stock performance. Renewable energy industry executives monitored the IPO closely because NexaGrid's success could influence broader sector sentiment.

Inside the company, employees followed every update obsessively.

Aaron understood that expectations were becoming dangerously high.

One evening after a particularly difficult day of meetings in London, Aaron sat alone inside his hotel room staring at the city lights outside the window.

He remembered the early days of NexaGrid vividly.

Back then, the company operated from a tiny office near an industrial warehouse district. Aaron personally handled software debugging, customer support calls, and investor pitches while struggling to make payroll.

Now global institutional investors debated whether the company deserved a multi-billion-dollar valuation.

The contrast felt surreal.

But Aaron also realized something equally important.

The roadshow was no longer about convincing investors the company existed. It was about convincing them the company could survive and grow responsibly as a public institution for years to come.

As the final week of the roadshow approached, investor demand strengthened significantly. Several large institutional funds increased their expected participation levels after meeting management repeatedly.

One pension fund manager explained the decision directly during a private conversation.

"The technology is impressive," she said. "But what really matters is that your team sounds realistic. Public markets punish leadership teams that promise fantasy outcomes."

That comment stayed with Aaron permanently.

When NexaGrid officially priced its IPO, the offering attracted strong institutional participation and significant investor demand. The stock performed well after listing, but unlike many hype-driven public offerings, NexaGrid maintained relatively stable trading because investor expectations aligned more realistically with operational execution.

Months later, Aaron spoke at a renewable energy leadership conference where another founder asked him what mattered most during the IPO roadshow.

"The numbers matter," Aaron answered. "The growth story matters. But ultimately, institutional investors invest in trust."

He paused briefly before continuing.

"During the roadshow, investors aren't just evaluating the company. They're evaluating how leadership behaves under pressure. They want to know whether you can communicate honestly when things go well—and when they don't."

Years later, NexaGrid became one of the most respected energy technology companies in global renewable infrastructure markets.

Looking back, Aaron often believed the IPO succeeded long before the stock began trading publicly.

It succeeded during those exhausting two weeks when institutional investors decided they trusted the leadership team enough to support the company through the unpredictable realities of public markets.

Because in the end, public companies are not built solely on products, revenue, or presentations.

They are built on confidence.

Chapter 8

The IPO Launch Day and Entering Public Markets

After years of preparation, financial audits, valuation discussions, regulatory filings, investor roadshows, and strategic planning, the company finally reaches one of the most symbolic and emotionally significant moments in its history—the IPO launch day. This is the moment when the company officially transitions from private ownership into the public markets. For founders, employees, early investors, and leadership teams, launch day often feels like the culmination of years of sacrifice, uncertainty, and relentless effort. Yet despite the excitement surrounding the public debut, the IPO launch is also one of the most delicate and strategically important moments in the company's evolution.

The IPO launch day is not simply a ceremonial event involving stock exchange bells and media attention. It is the point where investor demand, valuation strategy, public perception, and market psychology collide in real time. The company's stock price begins trading publicly, institutional investors receive share allocations, analysts evaluate market reaction, and the investing public forms its first impression of the company as a publicly traded entity. For many executives, IPO launch day begins long before the opening bell rings. Investment banks, legal teams, exchange officials, investor relations professionals, and executive leadership spend the final hours reviewing pricing decisions, investor allocations, trading expectations, media strategy, and market conditions carefully. Even at this late stage, market volatility, geopolitical news, economic data, or sudden investor sentiment changes can influence the launch environment significantly.

One of the most important decisions finalized before launch involves IPO pricing. After collecting institutional investor feedback during the roadshow process, underwriters and company leadership agree on the final offering price for shares. This pricing decision directly affects how much capital the company raises and how investors perceive future upside potential.

Pricing strategy is highly sensitive because the market immediately judges whether the IPO was priced appropriately. If the stock opens dramatically above the offering price, some may argue the company left money on the table by pricing too conservatively. If the stock performs poorly after listing, investors may conclude the offering was overpriced or that market enthusiasm was weaker than expected. Strong IPO launches usually balance investor demand with sustainable pricing. Companies that create healthy aftermarket trading momentum often establish stronger long-term investor confidence. Underwriters therefore attempt to structure pricing in ways that support both successful capital raising and positive market perception after trading begins.

Institutional investors receive most IPO share allocations initially. Large investment funds, pension funds, hedge funds, mutual funds, and asset managers typically purchase substantial portions of the offering before public trading begins. Underwriters carefully determine these allocations because they want stable long-term shareholders rather than speculative short-term traders dominating early ownership.

The quality of institutional shareholders can influence post-IPO stability significantly. Long-term investors focused on company fundamentals often create more stable trading environments compared to speculative investors seeking rapid short-term profits.

As the market opening approaches, media attention intensifies rapidly. Financial television networks broadcast live from stock exchanges. Journalists interview executives, analysts, and investors. Social media discussions accelerate. Employees, customers, competitors, and shareholders all watch closely as the company prepares to enter public markets officially. For founders, launch day often carries enormous emotional significance. Many entrepreneurs reflect on years of uncertainty, financial stress, operational struggles, investor rejection, product failures, hiring challenges, and personal sacrifice leading to this moment. What once existed only as an idea now becomes a publicly traded corporation visible to the entire financial world.

Yet behind the excitement, leadership teams often experience intense anxiety as well. Once trading begins, the market starts assigning real-time value to the company continuously. Public investors immediately begin reacting to valuation expectations, market sentiment, analyst opinions, and future growth assumptions.

When the opening bell finally rings and trading begins, market dynamics move extremely quickly. Buy orders, sell orders, institutional activity, retail investor demand, and trading algorithms all interact simultaneously. Early trading performance often receives enormous attention because it shapes public perception surrounding the IPO.

Strong first-day performance may create headlines celebrating the company's success and attract additional investor enthusiasm. Weak trading performance can create concerns regarding valuation, market timing, or investor confidence even if the underlying business remains fundamentally strong.

However, experienced executives understand that launch-day trading alone does not determine long-term success. Some companies experience explosive IPO openings but later struggle operationally. Others launch more modestly but build extraordinary long-term shareholder value through disciplined execution over many years.

This distinction is critical because public markets eventually focus far more on operational performance than launch-day excitement. Revenue growth, profitability, innovation, governance quality, customer retention, strategic execution, and leadership discipline ultimately matter far more than short-term trading volatility.

Another important dynamic during IPO launch day involves lock-up agreements. Executives, employees, and early investors are usually restricted from selling shares immediately after the IPO for a specified period, often around six months. These restrictions help stabilize trading and reduce sudden selling pressure during the company's early public market period.

Still, anticipation surrounding future insider sales often influences investor psychology after the IPO. Public markets closely monitor whether founders and early investors maintain confidence in the business after lock-up periods expire.

Analyst coverage also begins influencing market perception rapidly after launch. Investment banks and financial research firms publish opinions regarding valuation, growth potential, competitive positioning, and future earnings expectations. Positive analyst coverage may support investor enthusiasm, while cautious reports may influence trading pressure.

Public companies therefore enter an entirely new communication environment after launch day. Every earnings report, strategic announcement, acquisition, product launch, regulatory issue, leadership decision, and financial update becomes public information capable of influencing stock performance.

One of the biggest psychological adjustments founders face after launch day is learning how to separate stock price volatility from operational reality. Markets often react emotionally in the short term. Economic headlines, interest rate changes, investor sentiment shifts, geopolitical events, and speculative trading behavior may cause stock movement unrelated to the company's actual long-term business quality.

Founders who become emotionally consumed by daily stock fluctuations often struggle to maintain strategic focus. Strong public company leaders learn how to prioritize operational execution and long-term value creation rather than reacting impulsively to short-term market volatility.

Employees also experience major emotional changes after the IPO. Equity ownership suddenly becomes visible through publicly traded shares, creating excitement and financial optimism throughout the organization. Some employees may experience life-changing wealth creation almost overnight.

At the same time, stock visibility can also create distractions. Leadership teams must maintain organizational discipline and mission alignment despite increased financial focus inside the company.

Customers and business partners may also react differently after a company becomes public. Public status often improves credibility, strengthens branding, and increases market visibility. Some customers feel more confident working with publicly traded businesses because they perceive them as more stable, transparent, and financially secure.

Competitors, however, gain access to far more information once the company becomes public. Financial statements, growth metrics, strategic priorities, and operational details become visible through public filings and earnings reports. Public companies therefore sacrifice a degree of operational privacy in exchange for access to public capital markets.

Economic timing can significantly influence post-launch performance as well. Some companies launch during strong bullish markets where investor enthusiasm supports elevated valuations and aggressive growth expectations. Others face difficult environments involving economic uncertainty, inflation concerns, recession fears, or declining investor appetite for growth companies.

Even strong businesses can experience volatile trading if broader market conditions deteriorate after the IPO. This is why resilient leadership and disciplined execution matter so much after public listing.

One of the most important lessons regarding IPO launch day is understanding that public markets are driven heavily by perception and confidence. Investors evaluate not only historical financial performance but also future belief systems regarding the company's potential. Companies capable of sustaining investor trust through transparency, execution, and adaptability often perform better over time.

Public markets also reward consistency. Companies that repeatedly deliver predictable operational execution, clear communication, and disciplined capital allocation usually develop stronger institutional investor relationships and long-term shareholder support.

The IPO launch creates access to tremendous opportunities. Public capital can support acquisitions, infrastructure expansion, global scaling, product development, and strategic investment at levels rarely available within private markets. Yet these opportunities also create greater accountability and pressure.

Some founders struggle with the cultural transition after launch day. Public companies operate with more structure, governance, compliance obligations, and shareholder influence than many startup environments. Decision-making processes may become slower and more scrutinized. Public investors expect transparency, accountability, and financial discipline consistently.

Still, for companies prepared strategically, entering public markets can become transformational. Access to institutional capital, improved credibility, global visibility, acquisition flexibility, and shareholder liquidity can dramatically accelerate long-term business growth.

The launch day therefore represents both an ending and a beginning. It marks the conclusion of the private company phase while opening the door to the entirely different world of public markets.

The companies that ultimately succeed after launch day are usually not the ones most obsessed with opening-day headlines or temporary stock excitement. They are the ones focused on building durable businesses capable of executing consistently long after the media attention fades.

The opening bell may symbolize entry into public markets, but long-term success is determined by what the company does next.

The Morning Vantage AI Became Public

At 4:30 in the morning, Noah Carter was already awake.

He stood alone inside his New York hotel room staring out across the city skyline while the streets below remained mostly quiet. In just a few hours, Vantage AI Systems would officially become a publicly traded company.

The thought still felt surreal.

Only eight years earlier, Noah and his co-founder Elena Brooks had launched the company from a tiny apartment workspace with a single idea—using artificial intelligence to automate predictive supply chain optimization for global manufacturing companies.

Back then, survival itself seemed uncertain.

They spent years fighting through software failures, investor rejection, operational setbacks, and financial pressure. Noah personally maxed out credit cards to fund early development costs while Elena handled customer acquisition and technical infrastructure almost entirely by herself.

Now Wall Street analysts debated whether the company could become one of the largest enterprise AI businesses in the world.

At 6:00 AM, Noah arrived at Nasdaq headquarters alongside executives, underwriters, attorneys, and investor relations advisors. Financial media crews filled the building. Television screens displayed Vantage AI's ticker symbol repeatedly as commentators discussed the company's valuation and growth potential.

Employees began arriving shortly afterward, many wearing company-branded jackets and carrying phones already flooded with social media posts celebrating the IPO.

The excitement inside the room felt electric.

But beneath the excitement, Noah sensed enormous pressure.

The company had spent nearly two years preparing for this moment. Financial systems were rebuilt. SEC filings underwent endless revisions. Investor roadshows stretched across multiple countries. Analysts scrutinized every detail of the business.

Now the market would decide whether the company deserved its valuation. Inside a private conference room, the lead underwriter reviewed final pricing updates one last time.

“Demand remains strong,” he explained calmly. “Institutional allocations are fully covered.”

Elena leaned back quietly.

“What’s the expected opening range?”

The banker gave a slight smile.

“Likely higher than the offering price if market conditions stay stable this morning.”

The room relaxed slightly.

But Noah remained cautious.

He understood that opening-day enthusiasm could disappear quickly if the company failed to execute afterward.

At 8:30 AM, Noah and Elena appeared live on multiple financial news networks discussing the company’s future. Reporters asked about artificial intelligence trends, scalability opportunities, competition, and long-term profitability expectations. Noah answered carefully. For years, he imagined IPO day as pure celebration. Instead, he realized leadership responsibility felt even heavier now than during the startup years. Public investors were trusting the company with billions of dollars in capital and expectations.

At exactly 9:30 AM, surrounded by employees, executives, investors, and flashing cameras, Noah and Elena pressed the ceremonial button signaling the opening bell.

Applause erupted instantly.

Within minutes, Vantage AI's stock price surged above the offering price as institutional and retail investor demand accelerated rapidly.

Financial media celebrated the launch aggressively.

"AI IPO Success Story."

"One of the Year's Strongest Public Offerings."

"Wall Street Embraces Enterprise AI Growth."

Employees hugged each other emotionally as stock prices continued climbing throughout the morning. Early investors celebrated enormous returns. Some employees quietly realized their equity holdings had become life-changing financially overnight.

Yet even during the excitement, Noah noticed something important. Inside another conference room nearby, analysts and investors were already discussing future quarterly growth expectations, margin expansion potential, international scaling risks, and competitive threats.

The market had already moved beyond the IPO itself.

Public investors immediately focused on what came next.

That realization stayed with Noah throughout the day.

Late that afternoon, after most media interviews ended and employees returned to celebrations, Noah and Elena sat quietly inside a conference room overlooking Times Square.

"We did it," Elena said softly.

Noah nodded.

"Yes," he answered. "But now we have to stay worthy of it."

Over the following months, Noah discovered how different public company life truly was.

Analysts questioned every earnings report aggressively. Investors monitored growth metrics constantly. Media outlets reacted dramatically to even minor operational developments. The stock price fluctuated daily based on economic conditions, investor sentiment, and industry trends completely outside management's control. One quarter, Vantage AI exceeded revenue expectations significantly, and the stock surged. Another quarter, the company lowered future guidance slightly due to slower international expansion timelines, and the stock declined sharply despite strong long-term fundamentals.

Noah gradually learned that public markets were emotional, reactive, and often unpredictable in the short term.

But he also learned something more important.

The companies that survived public markets successfully focused less on stock volatility and more on building durable operational systems, strong customer relationships, and long-term strategic execution.

Years later, Vantage AI became one of the largest enterprise AI infrastructure companies in the world. The company expanded globally, acquired competitors, and continued innovating through changing technology cycles.

At an entrepreneurship summit, a founder once asked Noah what IPO day felt like.

Noah smiled thoughtfully before answering.

"It feels like crossing a finish line and realizing instantly that the real race is just beginning."

The audience laughed quietly.

"Going public gives you access to opportunity," he continued. "But it also gives the world permission to evaluate everything you do every single day afterward."

He paused briefly.

"The opening bell lasts a few seconds. The responsibility that follows can last decades."

Looking back, Noah realized the IPO launch was never truly about the stock exchange ceremony, headlines, or valuation alone.

It was about transition.

The moment Vantage AI stopped being simply a startup and became an institution expected to survive, grow, innovate, and create value under the constant pressure of public markets.

And in the end, that responsibility mattered far more than the excitement of opening day itself.

Chapter 9

Life After the IPO: Managing Public Markets, Shareholders, and Long-Term Expectations

For many entrepreneurs, the Initial Public Offering appears to be the ultimate finish line. Years of sacrifice, risk-taking, fundraising, operational scaling, and strategic execution finally culminate in the moment when the company begins trading publicly on a stock exchange. Financial media celebrates the offering. Employees watch stock prices rise in real time. Founders ring opening bells surrounded by cameras and investors. Wealth is created instantly on paper, and the business enters a completely new level of visibility and credibility.

Yet one of the most important realities of public markets is this: the IPO is not the end of the journey. In many ways, it is only the beginning.

The transition from private company to public corporation changes nearly every aspect of how a business operates. Public companies exist under continuous scrutiny from shareholders, analysts, institutional investors, regulators, media organizations, competitors, and the broader financial market.

The excitement surrounding the IPO may last for days or weeks, but eventually the market shifts its focus toward one thing above all else—execution.

Public investors expect companies to deliver on the promises made during the IPO process. Growth projections, expansion plans, profitability pathways, operational improvements, and strategic goals all become measurable expectations that shareholders monitor quarter after quarter. Companies that execute consistently often build long-term investor trust and sustainable shareholder value. Companies that fail to meet expectations may experience rapid stock declines, investor dissatisfaction, media criticism, and increased pressure from activist shareholders or institutional investors.

One of the biggest adjustments founders face after going public is the constant visibility of stock price movement. In private companies, business value may only be reassessed occasionally during funding rounds or acquisitions. Public companies, however, receive a real-time market valuation every trading day. Stock prices fluctuate constantly based on earnings reports, analyst opinions, economic conditions, investor sentiment, industry trends, interest rates, geopolitical events, and company-specific news. This constant feedback loop can become emotionally exhausting for leadership teams. Founders who once focused almost entirely on product development and long-term innovation may suddenly feel pressured by short-term market expectations. Every quarterly earnings report becomes a public performance evaluation capable of influencing billions of dollars in shareholder value within hours.

Quarterly reporting obligations become one of the defining realities of life as a public company. Public corporations must file regular financial reports detailing revenue, profitability, expenses, cash flow, risks, operational performance, and strategic developments. Investors analyze these reports intensely because they help determine whether the company is progressing according to expectations.

Earnings calls also become central events after the IPO. During these calls, executives discuss financial results and answer questions from analysts and institutional investors. Leadership communication quality matters enormously during these interactions because investors evaluate not only financial performance but also executive confidence, transparency, and strategic clarity.

Companies that communicate clearly and honestly often maintain stronger investor trust even during difficult periods. In contrast, leadership teams that avoid accountability, overpromise future performance, or communicate inconsistently may quickly lose credibility with the market.

Managing shareholder expectations becomes one of the most difficult challenges for newly public companies. During the IPO process, excitement and optimism often create elevated expectations regarding future growth. Investors may expect rapid expansion, margin improvement, international scaling, product innovation, and increasing profitability simultaneously.

However, business growth rarely follows perfectly smooth trajectories. Economic slowdowns occur. Competition intensifies. Operational challenges emerge. Hiring difficulties develop. Supply chains become disrupted. Technology evolves unexpectedly. Public companies must therefore balance ambitious growth strategies with realistic operational execution.

One of the most dangerous mistakes newly public companies make is focusing excessively on short-term stock performance instead of long-term business quality. Some leadership teams become obsessed with quarterly results and attempt to manage investor perception aggressively at the expense of strategic sustainability.

This short-term thinking can become destructive. Companies may reduce research and development spending, delay necessary investments, manipulate operational timing, or prioritize temporary earnings improvements instead of building durable long-term value. While such decisions may temporarily support stock prices, they often weaken the business over time.

Strong public companies usually maintain a long-term strategic mindset even while operating within short-term market environments. They understand that sustainable shareholder value ultimately depends on execution quality, operational discipline, innovation, customer satisfaction, and strategic adaptability rather than temporary stock volatility alone.

Investor relations becomes a permanent and highly important function after the IPO. Public companies maintain ongoing communication with institutional investors, analysts, shareholders, and financial media. Investor relations teams coordinate earnings calls, shareholder meetings, conferences, analyst presentations, financial disclosures, and market communication strategies.

The relationship between management and institutional investors evolves continuously after listing. Large shareholders may hold significant influence over company direction, especially if they control substantial ownership positions.

Institutional investors often provide feedback regarding strategy, governance, capital allocation, executive compensation, and long-term priorities.

Activist investors can also emerge after companies go public. Activist shareholders acquire ownership stakes and push aggressively for operational changes, leadership adjustments, acquisitions, asset sales, or financial restructuring designed to increase shareholder returns. Some activist campaigns create positive operational improvements, while others generate conflict and strategic instability.

Corporate governance therefore becomes increasingly important after the IPO. Public companies must maintain strong boards of directors, ethical compliance systems, executive accountability frameworks, and shareholder protections. Weak governance structures often lead to operational failures, financial scandals, or investor distrust.

Executive compensation also receives significant public attention after listing. Shareholders evaluate whether leadership incentives align appropriately with long-term shareholder interests. Compensation packages perceived as excessive or poorly structured can trigger investor criticism quickly.

Public companies also face increased legal exposure. Securities litigation, shareholder lawsuits, regulatory investigations, disclosure disputes, and compliance risks all become ongoing concerns. Companies must therefore maintain strong legal oversight and operational discipline to reduce exposure.

Media scrutiny intensifies dramatically after an IPO as well. Public companies operate under constant attention from financial journalists, industry analysts, social media discussions, and market commentators. Leadership decisions, operational setbacks, executive behavior, acquisitions, layoffs, cybersecurity incidents, and earnings performance all become highly visible.

This increased visibility creates both opportunity and risk. Positive media coverage can strengthen branding, investor confidence, and customer trust. Negative publicity can damage reputation rapidly and influence shareholder perception significantly.

Employee culture often changes substantially after companies go public. Stock-based compensation becomes more visible and emotionally influential because employees can monitor real-time market value fluctuations daily. Some employees become highly motivated by equity appreciation opportunities, while others become distracted by stock volatility or financial expectations. Leadership teams must therefore work intentionally to preserve company culture and operational focus after listing. Public market visibility should not replace innovation, customer service, teamwork, or long-term mission alignment.

Another important aspect of life after the IPO involves lock-up expiration periods. Early investors, executives, and employees are often restricted from selling shares immediately after the offering. Once lock-up periods expire, large share sales may create downward stock pressure or market concern regarding insider confidence.

Companies therefore manage these transitions carefully through investor communication and strategic planning.

Capital allocation becomes another central responsibility for public companies. Investors expect leadership teams to deploy capital intelligently through expansion investments, acquisitions, research and development, debt management, stock repurchases, or dividend strategies. Poor capital allocation decisions can weaken investor trust quickly.

Acquisitions often become more common after IPOs because public stock can be used as acquisition currency. Publicly traded shares allow companies to pursue strategic mergers and acquisitions more efficiently than many private businesses.

However, acquisition integration risks and overexpansion concerns also increase.

Economic cycles also influence post-IPO performance significantly. Many companies go public during strong market environments but later encounter recessions, interest rate increases, inflationary pressure, or sector downturns. Public investors evaluate whether leadership teams can adapt effectively during changing economic conditions.

Resilience becomes one of the most important qualities separating successful public companies from struggling ones. Markets reward businesses capable of maintaining strategic focus, operational discipline, and financial stability during difficult periods.

Technology and innovation pressures continue intensifying after the IPO as well. Public companies cannot rely solely on historical success. Competitors continue evolving, customer expectations change, and industries transform rapidly. Companies that stop innovating after going public often decline over time regardless of initial IPO success.

Founders also face personal identity transitions after the IPO. Some entrepreneurs struggle emotionally with the increased bureaucracy, governance requirements, investor pressure, and reduced operational flexibility associated with public companies. Others adapt successfully and evolve into highly effective public market leaders. Many founder-led public companies eventually transition leadership responsibilities to more operationally experienced executives capable of managing large-scale public corporations. These transitions can strengthen or destabilize companies depending on execution quality and cultural alignment.

Long-term wealth management becomes another major consideration for founders after IPOs. Large equity positions create both extraordinary opportunities and substantial risks. Founders must navigate diversification strategies, tax planning, liquidity management, estate planning, philanthropic decisions, and long-term financial sustainability carefully.

Despite the pressures of public markets, successful IPOs can create transformational opportunities. Public companies gain access to capital markets capable of supporting global expansion, technological innovation, infrastructure development, strategic acquisitions, and industry leadership positioning at scales rarely possible within private environments.

The companies that thrive after going public usually understand one critical principle: public markets reward consistency over time. Temporary excitement fades quickly. Sustainable execution, operational discipline, transparent communication, strategic adaptability, and long-term value creation ultimately determine whether a public company succeeds.

Life after the IPO therefore becomes a continuous test of leadership quality, organizational maturity, and strategic discipline. Companies that remain focused on building durable businesses rather than managing temporary market perceptions often create the greatest long-term shareholder value.

The IPO may open the door to public markets, but what happens afterward determines whether the company becomes a temporary headline or a lasting institution.

After the Bell: The Rise and Pressure of Solaris Motion

When Solaris Motion officially became a public company, CEO Marcus Hale stood on the balcony overlooking the trading floor trying to absorb what had just happened.

Only ten years earlier, he had started the company inside a rented industrial garage with three engineers and an idea for improving electric transportation systems through advanced battery optimization software. Now Solaris Motion had completed one of the largest clean transportation IPOs of the decade.

The company's stock surged nearly forty percent on its first trading day.

Financial media celebrated the offering relentlessly. Headlines described Marcus as one of the most influential entrepreneurs in the electric transportation industry. Employees watched their stock options explode in value. Venture capital investors celebrated enormous returns.

For a brief moment, everything felt perfect.

Then reality arrived.

The following Monday morning, Marcus entered headquarters expecting celebration and excitement. Instead, the executive team sat inside the conference room reviewing analyst reports discussing quarterly growth projections, manufacturing expansion risks, profitability expectations, and valuation concerns.

The stock market was already demanding more.

Within weeks, Marcus discovered how different public markets truly were from private company life.

As a private company, Solaris Motion focused heavily on long-term innovation. Product delays or temporary setbacks rarely became public crises. Investors remained patient because funding cycles occurred privately and infrequently.

Now every operational issue mattered immediately.

Production delays affected stock prices. Analyst downgrades triggered media criticism. Economic reports influenced investor sentiment daily. Competitor announcements impacted valuation. Public shareholders demanded constant transparency regarding expansion plans and profitability timelines.

The pressure became relentless.

Every quarter, Solaris Motion prepared earnings reports and investor presentations. Analysts questioned leadership aggressively about margins, manufacturing efficiency, battery supply chains, customer demand trends, and international expansion performance.

Marcus initially struggled emotionally with the environment.

One quarter, the company missed revenue expectations by a relatively small margin because of delayed battery shipments from overseas suppliers. The business itself remained fundamentally strong, but the stock price dropped sharply after the earnings announcement.

Financial media reacted dramatically.

"Has Solaris Motion Lost Momentum?"

"Can the Company Justify Its Valuation?"

"Growth Concerns Emerging in Electric Transportation Sector"

Marcus stared at the headlines late one evening feeling frustrated and exhausted.

The company had spent years building revolutionary technology and global infrastructure, yet public markets seemed obsessed with short-term fluctuations.

The next morning, Solaris Motion's Chairman of the Board requested a private conversation.

"You need to understand something," the Chairman explained calmly. "Public markets are emotional in the short term. Your job is not to react emotionally with them."

Marcus listened carefully.

"The companies that survive public markets learn how to separate temporary volatility from long-term strategy."

That advice changed Marcus's mindset completely.

Instead of obsessing over daily stock price movement, he began focusing more aggressively on operational execution, communication transparency, and long-term strategic discipline.

During the next earnings call, Marcus approached investor communication differently.

Rather than avoiding challenges or overpromising future results, he openly discussed supply chain disruptions, manufacturing improvements, and long-term expansion priorities realistically.

Investors responded positively.

One institutional shareholder later explained why.

"We don't expect perfection," the investor said. "We expect leadership teams capable of handling reality honestly."

As the years progressed, Solaris Motion continued facing constant public market pressure.

Competitors emerged aggressively. Economic slowdowns reduced investor enthusiasm for growth stocks periodically. Supply chain disruptions created operational volatility. Regulatory changes affected transportation infrastructure planning.

Yet the company remained resilient because leadership focused on building long-term durability instead of chasing temporary market approval.

Marcus also learned how important company culture became after the IPO.

Some employees became distracted by daily stock price fluctuations. Others developed unrealistic wealth expectations after the successful public offering. Internal pressure increased significantly as media attention and investor scrutiny intensified.

To maintain focus, Marcus emphasized the company's long-term mission repeatedly.

"We didn't build Solaris Motion for a stock symbol," he told employees during an internal meeting. "We built it to transform transportation infrastructure globally."

That cultural discipline helped stabilize the organization during difficult periods.

Several years after the IPO, Solaris Motion became one of the largest transportation technology companies in the world. The company expanded internationally, acquired competitors, and continued innovating within battery infrastructure and mobility systems.

At an entrepreneur conference, a founder once asked Marcus what surprised him most after going public.

Marcus smiled slightly before answering.

"The IPO itself was easier than staying public."

The audience laughed quietly.

"People think going public is the finish line," he continued. "In reality, it's the beginning of a completely different challenge. Public markets test your leadership every quarter. They test your patience, discipline, communication, and emotional control constantly."

He paused briefly.

"But if you stay focused on building a real company instead of managing daily stock emotions, public markets can become one of the most powerful growth platforms in the world."

Looking back, Marcus realized Solaris Motion's true success was not the IPO itself.

It was surviving everything that came afterward.

Because public companies are not ultimately judged by opening-day excitement.

They are judged by whether they can continue executing long after the cameras disappear and the market demands results year after year.

Chapter 10

Building Long-Term Wealth and Legacy Through Public Markets

For many entrepreneurs, the Initial Public Offering represents the beginning of extraordinary financial opportunity. Years of effort, risk, innovation, and strategic growth may suddenly convert into publicly tradable equity worth millions or even billions of dollars. Yet while IPOs often create dramatic wealth events, long-term financial success is not determined solely by the public offering itself. The real challenge begins after the IPO, when founders, executives, investors, and shareholders must decide how to preserve, grow, manage, and leverage wealth responsibly over time.

Public markets have historically created some of the greatest fortunes in modern history. Equity ownership in successful public companies has generated transformational wealth for founders, employees, institutional investors, venture capital firms, and long-term shareholders across industries ranging from technology and healthcare to manufacturing, finance, energy, and consumer products. Yet public markets have also destroyed wealth for those who lacked discipline, diversification, strategic planning, or long-term perspective. Understanding how to build lasting wealth through public markets therefore requires far more than understanding how to launch an IPO. It requires understanding capital allocation, equity management, long-term investing principles, tax strategy, risk management, diversification, legacy planning, and the psychology of wealth itself.

One of the first realities founders face after an IPO is that much of their wealth may initially remain concentrated in company stock. While this concentration can create enormous upside potential, it also creates significant risk. Many entrepreneurs become emotionally attached to their companies because the business represents years of sacrifice and identity. However, concentrated wealth positions can become financially dangerous if the company experiences market volatility, operational setbacks, competitive disruption, or economic downturns.

History contains countless examples of founders who became paper billionaires during strong market periods only to experience massive declines because too much personal wealth remained tied to a single stock. This is why diversification becomes one of the most important long-term wealth management principles after an IPO. Diversification does not mean abandoning belief in the company. It means recognizing that protecting long-term financial stability often requires reducing excessive concentration risk gradually over time.

Founders who diversify intelligently may preserve wealth more effectively across changing market cycles and economic conditions.

Tax planning also becomes critically important after public offerings. IPO-related wealth events can trigger substantial tax obligations depending on jurisdiction, equity structure, stock sale timing, and ownership arrangements. Capital gains taxes, income taxes, estate taxes, and liquidity planning all require careful strategic management.

Sophisticated founders and executives often work closely with tax attorneys, financial advisors, accountants, and estate planning professionals long before major liquidity events occur. Strategic planning may involve trusts, charitable foundations, donor-advised funds, family partnerships, long-term investment structures, and other financial planning vehicles designed to preserve and optimize wealth efficiently.

Liquidity management becomes another major challenge after IPOs. Public market wealth often appears enormous on paper, but liquidity restrictions, lock-up agreements, stock volatility, and tax considerations may limit immediate access to cash. Founders therefore need disciplined strategies regarding how and when to monetize portions of their holdings responsibly. Some founders make the mistake of selling too much stock too quickly after IPOs, which may signal lack of confidence to the market and reduce future upside participation. Others hold excessively concentrated positions for emotional reasons and expose themselves to unnecessary financial vulnerability. Balancing liquidity, diversification, and long-term ownership becomes one of the most important financial decisions after going public.

Public markets also create opportunities beyond personal wealth accumulation. Publicly traded stock can become a strategic asset used to fund acquisitions, support expansion initiatives, attract top talent through equity compensation, and strengthen long-term business growth. Founders who understand how to use equity strategically may continue building enterprise value long after the IPO itself.

Long-term shareholder value creation becomes another central focus after public listing. Sustainable public companies are built through disciplined capital allocation decisions over time. Investors evaluate how leadership teams deploy cash, pursue acquisitions, invest in innovation, manage debt, repurchase shares, or distribute dividends.

Companies that allocate capital intelligently often outperform over long periods because compounding effects become extremely powerful within public markets. Small strategic decisions repeated consistently over years may create extraordinary long-term shareholder value.

One of the most important wealth-building advantages of public markets is scalability. Public companies can raise additional capital through secondary offerings, convertible debt, institutional financing, or strategic partnerships more efficiently than many private businesses. This access to capital allows successful companies to expand globally, acquire competitors, accelerate innovation, and dominate industries at scale.

However, growth alone does not guarantee long-term wealth creation. Some companies pursue reckless expansion strategies that destroy shareholder value through excessive dilution, overleveraging, or poorly integrated acquisitions. Sustainable growth requires discipline, operational execution, and strategic clarity.

Public markets also reward patience. Many of the world's greatest fortunes were built not through short-term trading or rapid exits, but through decades of ownership in high-quality businesses. Compounding returns become extraordinarily powerful over time for companies capable of sustaining growth and innovation consistently. This principle applies not only to founders but also to long-term investors. Shareholders who identify durable businesses early and maintain conviction through market volatility often benefit significantly from compounding enterprise value over extended periods.

Market cycles represent another important consideration when building long-term wealth through public markets. Economic expansions, recessions, interest rate environments, inflationary periods, technological disruptions, and geopolitical events all influence stock performance over time. Investors and founders who understand market cycles often make more disciplined long-term decisions during periods of both optimism and fear.

One of the greatest dangers in public markets is emotional decision-making. Fear and greed drive enormous amounts of market behavior. During bullish environments, investors may become overconfident and ignore risk. During downturns, panic selling and pessimism may create poor long-term decisions.

Successful wealth builders often maintain emotional discipline during volatile periods. They focus on business fundamentals, operational quality, competitive positioning, and long-term value creation rather than reacting impulsively to short-term market noise.

Legacy planning becomes increasingly important as wealth grows through public market participation. Founders who create substantial wealth eventually begin considering broader questions beyond financial accumulation alone. How should wealth be preserved for future generations? What philanthropic goals matter most? How can wealth create positive long-term impact beyond personal lifestyle benefits?

Many public company founders establish charitable foundations, educational initiatives, research funding organizations, healthcare programs, environmental projects, or entrepreneurial mentorship efforts using wealth generated through equity ownership. Public market success therefore often creates opportunities for broader social influence and long-term legacy creation.

Family governance also becomes important for wealthy founders and executives. Multi-generational wealth preservation requires education, discipline, communication, and strategic planning. Without proper structures, significant wealth may disappear surprisingly quickly across future generations.

Public markets have also transformed entrepreneurship globally by creating pathways for wealth creation beyond traditional inheritance systems. Talented individuals capable of building scalable businesses can now create enormous value through innovation, leadership, and ownership participation regardless of background.

Technology has accelerated this process dramatically. Modern entrepreneurs can scale businesses globally faster than at any point in history. Software platforms, artificial intelligence, cloud infrastructure, digital marketplaces, and global communication networks allow companies to grow rapidly and access public capital markets earlier than previous generations could imagine.

Still, rapid wealth creation creates psychological challenges as well. Some founders struggle emotionally after IPOs because personal identity becomes heavily connected to stock performance, public perception, or financial comparisons. Others lose operational focus after achieving financial success.

The most effective long-term leaders usually maintain purpose beyond wealth itself. They continue focusing on innovation, impact, leadership, and building durable organizations rather than viewing the IPO as a final destination.

Another important reality is that public markets constantly evolve. Industries rise and fall. Technologies disrupt entire sectors. Regulatory environments shift. Investor preferences change. Companies that remain adaptable and innovative often sustain wealth creation across decades, while those that become complacent frequently decline. The relationship between innovation and long-term wealth cannot be overstated. Public markets reward companies capable of evolving continuously. Businesses that stop innovating eventually lose relevance regardless of previous success. Long-term wealth therefore depends not only on achieving market leadership but also on maintaining it through strategic adaptability.

Globalization has also expanded wealth creation opportunities significantly. Public companies now access international markets, global investor bases, multinational partnerships, and worldwide customer networks more efficiently than ever before. Companies capable of scaling globally may create value far beyond domestic market limitations.

Risk management remains equally important throughout this process. Public markets involve uncertainty permanently. Economic downturns, technological disruption, regulatory shifts, competitive threats, cyberattacks, geopolitical instability, and operational failures all create ongoing risks. Long-term wealth preservation therefore requires balancing growth ambition with financial resilience.

The greatest public market success stories are often built

through decades of disciplined execution rather than short-term speculation. Companies that prioritize customer value, operational quality, leadership integrity, innovation, and strategic discipline frequently create extraordinary long-term shareholder wealth over time.

For founders, the public markets provide something uniquely powerful—the ability to transform ownership into scalable, compounding, generational opportunity. Yet this opportunity comes with responsibility. Wealth without discipline may disappear quickly. Success without purpose may feel empty. Leadership without integrity eventually weakens trust.

Building long-term wealth and legacy through public markets therefore requires more than financial knowledge alone. It requires emotional discipline, strategic patience, operational excellence, thoughtful planning, and long-term vision.

The IPO may create the initial opportunity, but lasting wealth is built through what happens afterward—through decades of execution, adaptation, discipline, and purposeful leadership.

The Legacy Beyond the IPO: The Story of Atlas Quantum

When Atlas Quantum Technologies completed its IPO, financial media immediately declared founder Victor Reynolds one of the newest billionaires in the artificial intelligence industry.

The headlines spread everywhere.

"Quantum AI Founder Joins Billionaire Ranks."

"One of the Largest Tech IPOs of the Decade."

"Atlas Quantum Redefines Predictive Computing."

Investors celebrated massive gains as the company's stock surged during its first months of public trading. Employees who once worked inside a tiny office above an old warehouse suddenly held stock positions worth millions of dollars. Venture capital firms achieved extraordinary returns on early investments.

From the outside, it looked like the perfect success story.

But privately, Victor felt strangely unsettled.

For over twelve years, every part of his life revolved around building Atlas Quantum. The company developed advanced predictive artificial intelligence systems capable of optimizing industrial logistics, financial forecasting, and energy infrastructure management at unprecedented scale.

The journey consumed nearly everything.

Victor sacrificed relationships, sleep, financial stability, and personal comfort for years while building the company. He survived multiple near-bankrupt periods, investor rejection, technology failures, and operational crises before Atlas Quantum finally succeeded.

Now, after the IPO, he technically possessed more money than he could reasonably spend in several lifetimes.

Yet instead of relief, he felt pressure.

The company's stock price fluctuated daily under intense media attention. Institutional investors demanded aggressive expansion. Analysts debated valuation constantly. Public expectations seemed endless.

One evening, several months after the IPO, Victor sat quietly inside his office reviewing financial reports while the city lights glowed outside the windows.

His Chief Financial Officer entered carrying a stack of documents.

"We need to discuss diversification planning," she said carefully.

Victor barely looked up.

"You mean selling stock."

She nodded. "You've built enormous wealth," she explained. "But almost all of it is still concentrated in Atlas Quantum shares."

Victor leaned back silently.

Emotionally, the idea of selling stock felt almost disloyal. Atlas Quantum represented his life's work. Yet intellectually, he understood the risk.

The CFO continued.

"Public markets are unpredictable. Even great companies experience volatility. You need long-term protection, not just concentrated exposure."

Over the following months, Victor began working closely with financial advisors, tax attorneys, and wealth strategists for the first time in his life.

The process changed how he viewed wealth completely.

Before the IPO, money represented survival and growth capital. After the IPO, wealth became something different entirely—a responsibility requiring strategy, discipline, and long-term thinking.

Victor gradually diversified portions of his holdings into broader investments, real estate, infrastructure projects, and long-term global funds. He established trusts designed to preserve wealth across future generations. He created a charitable foundation focused on artificial intelligence education and technological access for underserved communities.

At first, many investors criticized his philanthropy efforts.

"Why give away so much capital during expansion years?" one analyst questioned publicly.

Victor ignored the criticism.

For the first time, he began thinking beyond quarterly earnings reports and stock performance.

He began thinking about legacy.

Meanwhile, Atlas Quantum continued growing aggressively. The company expanded internationally, acquired competitors, and entered new industries through advanced AI applications.

But public market life remained emotionally intense.

One year, economic recession fears caused technology stocks to collapse broadly. Atlas Quantum's valuation dropped sharply despite continued operational growth. Financial media questioned whether AI valuations had become excessive.

Employees panicked internally as stock prices declined. Victor called an emergency company-wide meeting.

“We cannot build this company based on market emotions,” he told employees firmly. “The mission has not changed because the stock price changed.”

That discipline became critical.

While weaker competitors cut innovation spending aggressively during the downturn, Atlas Quantum continued investing heavily in research and infrastructure. Several years later, those investments positioned the company far ahead of competitors when market conditions improved again.

The experience taught Victor one of the most important lessons of public markets.

Long-term wealth is rarely built through emotional reactions.

It is built through disciplined decisions repeated consistently over time.

Years later, Atlas Quantum became one of the world’s most influential artificial intelligence infrastructure companies. The business generated enormous shareholder value across decades rather than quarters.

But what mattered most to Victor eventually had little to do with personal net worth alone. His educational foundation funded thousands of engineering scholarships globally. Research partnerships accelerated technological innovation in healthcare and renewable energy systems. Entrepreneur mentorship programs helped young founders from disadvantaged backgrounds launch companies of their own.

One afternoon, while speaking at a global entrepreneurship summit, Victor was asked a simple question.

"What did the IPO ultimately give you?"

The audience expected him to discuss wealth.

Instead, Victor paused thoughtfully before answering.

"Freedom," he said quietly.

The room became silent.

"Not freedom to buy things," he continued. "Freedom to think long term. Freedom to create opportunities for other people. Freedom to build something larger than myself."

He looked across the audience carefully.

"Money matters. Ownership matters. Public markets matter. But eventually, every founder has to decide whether wealth is the final goal—or simply a tool." Years later, financial historians often described Atlas Quantum as one of the defining AI companies of its generation. But those closest to Victor understood something deeper.

The company's greatest success was not the IPO itself.

It was what happened afterward.

Because true legacy is rarely built through one extraordinary financial event alone.

It is built through decades of disciplined leadership, purposeful decisions, and the willingness to use success to create lasting value far beyond personal wealth.

Final IPO Thoughts

Taking a company public is one of the most ambitious and transformative journeys an entrepreneur, executive team, or investor can experience. Throughout this book, we explored the complete roadmap of a traditional Initial Public Offering, from understanding how companies enter public markets to preparing financial systems, building governance structures, selecting investment banks, preparing SEC filings, determining valuation strategies, conducting investor roadshows, and navigating life after the IPO. Yet beyond the technical processes and financial mechanics lies a much deeper reality about what public markets truly represent.

An IPO is not simply a transaction.

It is a transformation.

The process of becoming a public company changes the structure, responsibilities, visibility, and future trajectory of a business forever. Private companies often operate with flexibility, speed, and limited external oversight. Public companies operate inside a far more demanding environment shaped by institutional investors, regulatory obligations, shareholder expectations, market psychology, and continuous performance evaluation. The companies that thrive in this environment are rarely the ones that simply move fastest. They are usually the ones that prepare most thoroughly, lead most strategically, and execute most consistently over time.

One of the most important lessons throughout the IPO journey is that preparation creates confidence. Investors may become excited about disruptive technology, rapid growth, or market opportunity, but long-term institutional support is built upon trust. Public investors want confidence that leadership understands the business deeply, manages capital responsibly, communicates transparently, and possesses the discipline necessary to navigate uncertainty. This trust is not created overnight. It is earned gradually through operational maturity, financial transparency, governance quality, and strategic consistency.

Founders often begin companies with bold visions and enormous personal sacrifice. In the early stages, survival itself may feel uncertain. Entrepreneurs work through financial stress, operational challenges, hiring difficulties, product failures, investor rejection, and constant pressure while attempting to build something valuable enough to survive in competitive markets. Most startups never reach profitability. Far fewer ever become IPO candidates. Reaching the public market stage therefore represents a remarkable achievement already. However, one of the biggest misconceptions surrounding IPOs is the belief that becoming public automatically guarantees long-term success or permanent wealth. History has repeatedly shown that some companies experience massive IPO excitement only to struggle afterward because the underlying business lacked durability, discipline, or sustainable operational execution. Public markets eventually expose weaknesses. Hype may create temporary valuations, but only execution creates lasting shareholder value.

This is why the strongest companies focus on building real businesses long before pursuing public offerings. They prioritize operational systems, scalable infrastructure, leadership quality, financial discipline, customer satisfaction, and long-term strategy rather than chasing short-term headlines alone. Companies that build durable foundations usually perform better not only during IPOs but also throughout the years following public listing.

Another critical lesson is that valuation should never become the sole objective. During strong market environments, founders and investors may become emotionally attached to achieving the highest possible valuation. Yet excessively aggressive pricing often creates dangerous expectations that become difficult to sustain once quarterly reporting begins. Sustainable public market success usually depends less on maximizing opening-day excitement and more on building investor confidence over years of consistent execution.

Public markets reward companies capable of adapting continuously. Industries evolve, technologies shift, customer behavior changes, competitors emerge, regulations evolve, and economic cycles fluctuate constantly. Businesses that stop innovating after going public often decline regardless of how successful the IPO itself appeared initially. The companies that become lasting institutions are usually those that remain disciplined, resilient, and adaptable long after public listing.

Leadership also changes significantly after the IPO. Founders who once focused primarily on product innovation and operational growth must now communicate effectively with institutional investors, analysts, regulators, shareholders, media organizations, and global financial markets. Public company leadership requires emotional discipline because executives face constant scrutiny and pressure from both markets and shareholders.

The emotional side of public markets is often underestimated. Stock prices fluctuate daily based on countless variables outside management's direct control. Economic reports, interest rates, geopolitical tensions, investor sentiment, analyst commentary, industry trends, and competitor announcements can all influence valuation rapidly. Leadership teams that become emotionally reactive to short-term market volatility often make poor long-term decisions. Strong executives learn how to remain strategically focused even while markets fluctuate unpredictably around them.

The relationship between public markets and wealth creation is another important theme throughout the IPO process. Public offerings can create extraordinary financial opportunities for founders, employees, early investors, and shareholders. Equity ownership has historically been one of the most powerful wealth-building mechanisms in modern economic systems. Many of the world's most successful entrepreneurs created transformational wealth through ownership in publicly traded businesses.

Yet wealth creation through IPOs also requires responsibility. Founders who suddenly gain enormous liquidity must navigate tax planning, diversification strategies, long-term capital preservation, philanthropy decisions, and personal identity transitions carefully. Many entrepreneurs discover that financial success alone does not automatically create fulfillment or stability. Long-term wealth management therefore becomes just as important as wealth creation itself.

Employees also experience major transitions after IPOs. Equity compensation may become highly valuable, changing financial expectations and workplace culture dramatically. Leadership teams must preserve organizational focus, innovation, and mission alignment despite increased market visibility and financial pressure. Public companies that lose their internal culture often struggle to maintain long-term performance consistency.

One of the strongest themes repeated throughout the IPO journey is the importance of transparency. Public markets depend on disclosure, accountability, and investor trust. Companies that communicate honestly about risks, challenges, opportunities, and strategic priorities generally build stronger long-term credibility. Investors do not expect perfection. They expect leadership teams capable of understanding reality clearly and responding intelligently.

The IPO process itself often strengthens companies even before shares begin trading publicly. Preparing financial systems, governance structures, reporting controls, investor communication strategies, and operational infrastructure forces businesses to mature rapidly. Many companies become significantly stronger organizations simply by preparing for public market standards.

Institutional investors also play a larger role in public markets than many founders initially understand. Long-term shareholders often provide stability, strategic insight, and capital support during both strong and difficult periods. Building healthy relationships with institutional investors therefore becomes an important long-term leadership responsibility after listing.

At the same time, companies must avoid becoming overly dependent on short-term investor approval. Some businesses damage themselves by prioritizing quarterly earnings expectations at the expense of long-term innovation or operational investment. Sustainable public companies balance market accountability with strategic patience.

Technology continues reshaping capital markets as well. Artificial intelligence, digital trading systems, global communication platforms, retail investor participation, and advanced financial analytics have transformed how companies interact with markets. Future IPO environments may look very different from those of previous decades, but the core principles of trust, execution, governance, and operational quality will likely remain constant.

The future of public markets will also continue evolving globally. Emerging industries such as artificial intelligence, biotechnology, renewable energy, cybersecurity, robotics, blockchain infrastructure, space technology, and advanced automation may create entirely new categories of IPO opportunities. Entrepreneurs capable of building scalable, innovative, and disciplined organizations within these sectors may shape the next generation of public market leaders.

Still, regardless of industry or market cycle, the companies most likely to succeed publicly are those that understand a fundamental truth: an IPO is not the goal. Building a durable business is the goal.

The IPO is simply a financing and ownership transition that may accelerate growth opportunities if managed correctly.

Some of the greatest public companies in history succeeded not because they had the most exciting IPOs, but because they continued executing long after the initial excitement faded. They adapted during recessions, survived competitive pressure, innovated through changing industries, strengthened customer relationships, allocated capital intelligently, and maintained investor trust across decades rather than quarters.

This perspective is especially important for founders. Public markets may create fame, wealth, and visibility, but they also create responsibility. Once a company becomes public, leadership decisions affect employees, shareholders, pension funds, institutions, customers, and communities globally. Public corporations influence economies, industries, and lives at enormous scale.

The companies that leave the greatest legacy are often those that combine financial success with long-term value creation, innovation, integrity, and disciplined leadership.

As you reflect on the lessons throughout this book, remember that every IPO story begins long before Wall Street, stock exchanges, investment banks, or media attention become involved. It begins with a founder willing to solve a problem, build a vision, endure uncertainty, and continue pushing forward despite setbacks.

The public markets simply magnify what the company already is.

If leadership lacks discipline, markets eventually expose it. If governance is weak, investors eventually notice. If operational systems cannot scale, performance eventually declines. But if a company builds strong foundations, communicates transparently, adapts intelligently, and executes consistently, public markets can become one of the most powerful engines for long-term expansion and wealth creation ever created.

The IPO journey ultimately teaches a larger lesson about business itself.

Success is rarely created through one moment alone.

It is created through years of disciplined preparation, strategic thinking, operational consistency, emotional resilience, and long-term execution.

The opening bell may mark the beginning of public trading, but true success is determined by everything the company does afterward.

For entrepreneurs, investors, executives, and future founders, understanding the IPO process provides far more than financial knowledge. It provides insight into how modern capital markets reward trust, discipline, innovation, and long-term vision. Whether your future involves building a public company, investing in IPOs, advising businesses, or simply understanding how wealth is created through equity markets, the lessons within this journey can shape the way you think about business, leadership, ownership, and opportunity for years to come.

The road from private company to public corporation is difficult, unpredictable, and demanding.

But for those prepared to navigate it strategically, it can also become one of the most transformative journeys in modern business and wealth creation.

www.ingramcontent.com/pod-product-compliance
Lightning Source LLC
LaVergne TN
LVHW040518210926
848480LV00007BA/1508
* 9 7 9 8 2 5 6 0 1 5 3 7 4 *